BRETHREN
NEW TESTAMENT
COMMENTARY

1 CORINTHIANS

Harold S. Martin

```
227.2 M364f
Martin, Harold S., 1930-
1 Corinthians
```

BRF
PUBLISHED BY
Brethren Revival Fellowship
Ephrata, Pennsylvania

ISBN 0-9745027-2-3

Unless otherwise noted, all scripture quotations will be in the New King James Version.

Copyright 2004 by Brethren Revival Fellowship
All rights reserved
Printed in the United States of America

Copies of this book are available from:
Brethren Revival Fellowship
P. O. Box 543
Ephrata, PA 17522

GENERAL PREFACE

This commentary is part of a new series of studies that will feature a number of volumes covering all of the New Testament books. There will be reliable expositions of the Bible text, a careful analysis of key words, easy outlines to follow, and helpful material to aid serious Bible students. The explanations are written from a conservative evangelical Brethren and Anabaptist point of view. The goal is to expound the Bible text accurately, and to produce a readable explanation of God's truth.

Each volume can be especially useful for pastors, Sunday School teachers, and lay persons. The writers aim for thoroughness, clarity, and loyalty to the Anabaptist/Pietist values. The meaning of the Greek text (both for those who know Greek and those who don't), will be part of the exposition when necessary.

The *Brethren New Testament Commentary* sponsored by Brethren Revival Fellowship, will simply take the biblical text as it is, and give the exposition along with applications for everyday life. All who have been asked to write the commentaries in this series agree that the message of God's Word in its original documents was given without error, and that nothing more is necessary for spiritual growth.

Brethren Revival Fellowship is a renewal movement within the *Church of the Brethren* which aims to proclaim and preserve biblical values for living today. We believe the Bible is the infallible Word of God, the final authority for belief and practice, and that to personally accept Jesus Christ as Savior is the only means of salvation.

The Brethren Revival Fellowship Committee

This book is dedicated to
our oldest daughter,
Christine Faye Newcomer.
We remember how you brightened
our home and never gave us reason
to be ashamed. Now Dale Newcomer has become your
good husband and you have a family of your own.
May the lives of each member of your family
model obedience to the teachings found in
1 Corinthians.

FOREWORD
The Book of 1 Corinthians

The *Brethren New Testament Commentary* series aims to give a reliable and readable explanation of the New Testament text, with loyalty to Anabaptist and Pietist values. The Anabaptists and Pietists in Europe took the matter of biblical inspiration and authority for granted. They searched the Word of God carefully, and sought to avoid the error of "selective obedience." They tried earnestly to obey all the instructions of Christ and His apostles—not to gain favor with God, but to please the Lord in all of life.

The church at Corinth was established by Paul on his second missionary journey (Acts 18:1-17). It was largely a Gentile church, although Paul began his ministry in the synagogue, and some Jews responded to the gospel message. The synagogue ministry was brought to a halt when some Jews appealed to the governor for help in stopping the Apostle. Paul, however, was able to continue his ministry in the home of "a certain man named Justus," whose house was next door to the synagogue—and so he spent the better part of two years in Corinth.

Sometime later Paul learned from persons who were members of "Chloe's household" (1 Corinthians 1:11), about some difficulties which had arisen in the Corinthian church. At a later time, Paul received a letter from the church in which they requested answers to a number of questions (1 Corinthians 7:1). And so there were a number of problems that troubled the believers in the young church at Corinth. It was that information that led to the writing of the epistle.

The book of 1 Corinthians gives us a good picture of the life of the early church. It deals with Christian conduct. It is essentially an epistle of correction. Brethren Elder I.N.H.

Beahm appropriately called the epistle "a straight letter to a crooked church."

The study in this commentary on *1 Corinthians* is an attempt to explain and apply the teaching in the text. It has been a joy to work on preparing these studies which are designed to teach the Word of God to others through organization, exposition, and application of the Bible message. A special word of thanks is extended to David and Carolyn Kent, Martha Hess, and my wife Priscilla, for their help in proof-reading the manuscript.

This commentary is divided into thirteen chapters, and therefore it could be used as a textbook for a series of weekly lessons during a calendar quarter.

It is my hope that the expositions and applications of the Bible text found in this commentary will be a great blessing to preachers, to Christian workers, to young people, to parents in the home, and to all who set out to study the New Testament Scriptures.

I suggest that you keep your Bible open while you use the pages of this commentary. It is my prayer that you will have a delightful and helpful experience. To study the Bible is our highest privilege. To obey it is our greatest responsibility. To share its message with others is to participate in bringing lasting joy to many hungry hearts.

Those who teach Bible classes and those who preach the Word may feel free to use any part of these studies which they find helpful. May God use this book to encourage many hearts, to help steer believers from error, and to bring souls to the Savior, our Lord Jesus Christ.

Harold S. Martin
26 United Zion Circle
Lititz, PA 17543

TABLE OF CONTENTS
Book of 1 Corinthians

Page
    7—Foreword
    11—Introduction to 1 Corinthians

15 Chap 1—Divisions around Persons (1:1-17)
    15—The Saints in Corinth (1:1-9)
    20—The Exhortation to Unity (1:10-17)

27 Chap 2—The Gospel and the Intellectual (1:18-3:4)
    27—False Wisdom and the Gospel (1:18-31)
    33—The Nature of Christian Preaching (2:1-5)
    37—True Wisdom and the Spirit (2:6-3:4)

47 Chap 3—The Role of Faithful Ministers (3:5-4:21)
    47—The Apostles as Co-workers with God (3:5-23)
    53—An Evaluation of God's Ministers (4:1-5)
    55—The Low Estate of God's Ministers (4:6-13)
    58—The Concern of God's Ministers (4:14-21)

61 Chap 4—Maintaining Church Discipline (5:1-13)
    61—The Occasion for Church Discipline (5:1-3)
    64—The Necessity for Church Discipline (5:4-8)
    66—The Grounds for Church Discipline (5:9-11)
    68—The Dangers of Church Discipline (5:12-13)

71 Chap 5—Lawsuits and Moral Purity (6:1-20)
    71—The Scandal of Going to Law (6:1-4)
    73—The Remedy Instead of Going to Law (6:5-8)
    75—Violations of Christian Moral Standards (6:9-17)
    81—The Practice of True Christian Liberty (6:18-20)

85 Chap 6—Faithful Marriage (7:1-40)
    85—Principles for Married Life (7:1-9)
    89—Regulations for the Married Believer (7:10-16)
    93—Further Counsel on Marriage (7:17-40)

101 Chap 7—Christian Liberty (8:1-10:33)
    101—Food Sacrificed to Idols (8:1-13)
    106—Paul's List of Ministry Rights (9:1-14)
    110—Paul's Limits to Rights of Ministry (9:15-27)
    115—The Danger of Self-Confidence (10:1-22)
    123—Limits to Spiritual Freedom (10:23-33)

127 Chap 8—Head Coverings & the Lord's Supper (11:1-34)
    127—The Veiling of Women (11:1-16)
    135—Disorders at the Lovefeast (11:17-34)

141 Chap 9—Using Spiritual Gifts (12:1-31)
    141—The Diversity of Spiritual Gifts (12:1-11)
    146—The Importance of All Gifts (12:12-31)

153 Chap 10—The Way of Love (13:1-13)
    154—The Supremacy of Love (13:1-3)
    156—The Character of Love (13:4-7)
    161—The Durability of Love (13:8-13)

165 Chap 11—Tongues and Prophecy (14:1-40)
    165—The Superiority of Prophecy over Tongues (14:1-6)
    169—Limitations on Speaking in Tongues (14:7-25)
    174—Regulations for Worship in the Church (14:26-40)

183 Chap 12—Bodily Resurrection (15:1-58)
    183—The Importance of the Resurrection (15:1-19)
    187—The Order of Future Resurrections (15:20-34)
    193—The Nature of the Resurrection Body (15:35-50)
    198—The Bodies of the Transformed Living (15:51-58)

203 Chap 13—Conclusion: Personal Matters (16:1-24)
    203—Collection for the Poor at Jerusalem (16:1-4)
    205—Planning for a Prospective Journey (16:5-9)
    206—Exhortations for Christian Workers (16:10-18)
    209—The Salutation and Closing Words (16:19-24)

    213—Review Questions
    219—Bibliography

INTRODUCTION TO 1 CORINTHIANS

The letter known as 1 Corinthians was written by the Apostle Paul to the Christians in the church at Corinth. The message is intended for believers everywhere who gather in all places to call upon the name of the Lord.

Corinth is a city in Greece. Paul had been at Athens for a few months toward the end of A.D. 51. Only a few converts for Christ were won there (Acts 17:34). He left Athens for Corinth and found lodging there with Priscilla and Aquila. Paul preached in the synagogue at Corinth with some success, and stayed in Corinth for the better part of two years (Acts 18:11)—longer than in any other city except for his time at Ephesus. Paul is credited with being the founder of the church at Corinth.

Corinth is located in the southern part of Greece, on a land formation which is nearly an island. The southern part of the country (Achaia) is connected to the northern part (Macedonia) by a narrow neck of land only four miles wide. Corinth is built on that narrow isthmus. This location made it inevitable that Corinth should become one of the greatest trading and commercial centers in the ancient world.

All north-south traffic in Greece passed through Corinth; there was no other way for it to go. The greater part of east-west traffic passed through Corinth because the southern tip of Greece was a dangerous area for sailing vessels. And so instead of sailing around the southern portion of Achaia, ships entered the harbor at Corinth on one side of the city; the cargo was disembarked and carried by porters across the isthmus, and placed on another ship on the other side. The brief trip across the isthmus saved more than 200 miles of sailing around the most dangerous cape of the Mediterranean.

Corinth in New Testament times was the largest city in Greece. It was populated by many diverse groups of people. There were *Greeks* who delighted in shallow philosophy; there were *priestesses* attached to the temple of Aphrodite (the goddess of lust and carnal love); there were *Roman families* (sent by Julius Caesar to help rebuild Corinth); there were *traders* from Asia and Italy (seamen and merchants). Multitudes of people from a variety of backgrounds populated the city of Corinth—Romans, Greeks, Orientals, Jews, vagabonds, merchants, fortune-hunters, and pleasure-seekers.

The people who lived in Corinth for the most part were Gentiles. Immorality and drunkenness were rampant in the city. Corinth was the Las Vegas of the ancient world. Undoubtedly the church was impacted by the society in which it existed. As indicated in the *Foreword* to this book (on page 7), Paul had heard about the state of the Corinthian church through some people from "Chloe's household" (1 Corinthians 1:11). Also, the church had addressed a letter of inquiry to Paul (1 Corinthians 7:1). The epistle known as 1 Corinthians is Paul's response in light of those two developments.

The book of 1 Corinthians is sometimes contrasted with the book of Romans. Romans is a theological treatise on God's plan of redemption; 1 Corinthians is a letter calling for upright conduct in the lives of those who have chosen to follow Jesus Christ.

The book of Romans begins with the old nature; First Corinthians begins with the new nature.

The book of Romans requires justification; First Corinthians requires sanctification.

The book of Romans leads sinners to Christ; First Corinthians leads Christians to Christlikeness.

The book of Romans presents the appeal of a new faith; First Corinthians presents an appeal for faithfulness.

To understand and apply the teachings found in the epistle known as *1 Corinthians* should be one of the highest goals of every believer in the Lord Jesus Christ.

Chapter 1

DIVISIONS AROUND PERSONS
1 Corinthians 1:1-17

Corinth was a bustling maritime city in Greece. It had a reputation for licentiousness and immorality of all sorts. Since most of the converts came from a non-Jewish background, they were not familiar with the Old Testament laws and practices. They needed instruction and help as they moved from the ethical standards of the pagan society to those of the Christian life.

Numerous problems beset the young believers at Corinth. The church was divided into competing factions: some were suing each other at the law; there was a case of abominable immorality; problems relating to marriage and divorce troubled the church. Questions about the role of women, the Lord's Supper, and spiritual gifts plagued the congregation. In 1 Corinthians, Paul addressed these issues and gave some principles that are instructions for God's people down through the ages.

1. The Saints in Corinth (1:1-9)
The first nine verses of Paul's letter to the Corinthians contain a salutation and greeting.

(1:1) Paul, called to be an apostle of Jesus Christ through the will of God, and Sosthenes our brother,

The writer is Paul, a Jew from the tribe of Benjamin, a descendant of Abraham (2 Corinthians 11:22). Paul was born in Tarsus, raised a Pharisee, and educated in Jerusalem under Gamaliel (Acts 22:3).

In 1 Corinthians, Paul followed the format of most First Century writers. He began the letter by introducing himself as one called on a special mission (*an apostle*), who was chosen by "the will of God." Paul had not chosen the apostleship; God had chosen him. Paul had heard God's call on the Damascus Road.

Sosthenes was likely Paul's secretary who wrote the letter as Paul dictated the information to him. He may have been the Jewish synagogue leader named in Acts 18:17, one who had now become a Christian.

(1:2) To the church of God which is at Corinth, to those who are sanctified in Christ Jesus, called to be saints, with all who in every place call on the name of Jesus Christ our Lord, both theirs and ours:

The "church of God which is at Corinth" indicates that wherever an individual congregation is located, it is a fragment of the one universal "church of God."

By addressing the letter to "all who in every place call on the name of Jesus Christ"—Paul was making it clear that although this letter was dealing with specific issues facing Corinth, *all believers* are expected to learn from (and abide by) the instructions found here. The message found in 1 Corinthians is not for the church at Corinth alone; it is for every Christian down through the years.

To "those who are sanctified in Christ Jesus" is a reference to the fact that believers, upon accepting Christ, are chosen and set apart by Christ for His service. There are several aspects of sanctification.

Positional sanctification is a setting apart by Christ at the time of conversion (Hebrews 10:10; Acts 26:18). Positional sanctification is a state into which believers are brought by the new birth.

Progressive sanctification speaks of spiritual growth which occurs when the Holy Spirit instructs us through the Scriptures (Ephesians 5:26; John 17:17).

Progressive sanctification is an experience which becomes a daily process as we grow in Christ Jesus.

The phrase "called to be saints"—could be stated as "called to be holy." For Paul to speak of the "saints" at Corinth seems unusual in light of their many problems, and the evidence of carnality in their lives. In the New Testament, Christians are called by four names:

"saints" for their holiness
"believers" for their faith
"brethren" for their love
"disciples" for their obedience

The word "saints" refers to those who are separated from the world, and are set apart for God as holy.[1] Christians are expected to live their lives in accord with values that differ from the world's standards.

The church at Corinth had many weaknesses and faults, but still Paul could say of the young believers there that they have been "sanctified in Christ Jesus." This means that they now were members of God's family, but all through the letter there is a call for a human response—a need to strive further after holiness.

(1:3) Grace to you and peace from God our Father and the Lord Jesus Christ.

Paul used the two words "grace" and "peace" as a standard greeting in nearly all his letters.

"Grace" is God's undeserved favor and kindness. Grace is God's love in action, empowering those whom God regards with favor. Grace not only *saves* (Ephesians 2:8), but God's grace also *sustains* in the midst of the trials of life (Hebrews 4:16).

---

[1] The word "saints" was a common designation for New Testament Christians. The use of the word to describe people who were considered the "spiritual elite" only surfaced in later centuries.

"Peace" is harmony between the soul and God. Peace is freedom from guilt, hostility, and anxiety. To a church torn by internal dissensions, this initial prayer for peace was especially appropriate.

(1:4) I thank my God always concerning you for the grace of God which was given to you by Christ Jesus,

Paul's pattern was generally to follow his greeting with words of thanksgiving. To the Christians at Corinth, he was able to express thanks in spite of the reports he had heard about them.

Paul used good psychology in that he was not blind to the good qualities of the people to whom he was writing. Paul knew about the creeping worldliness, the gross immorality, and the selfish divisions at Corinth—but regardless of their shortcomings, there were some good things to be said, and Paul commended the people for those good things. Some people tend to see only the dark side of almost every situation. Paul was not the kind of person who focused merely on the negative.

(1:5-6) that you were enriched in everything by Him in all utterance and all knowledge, even as the testimony of Christ was confirmed in you,

It was the grace of God which "enriched" the believers at Corinth, giving them gifts for service, and strength to stand against the paganism and immorality of the Corinthian population.

The word "utterance" speaks of "the power of outward expression." The Greeks had for centuries been famous as speakers and thinkers. The people at Corinth had something to say, and they had the gift of speech so that they could say it well. The message of the gospel seems to have given them an even richer ability to express God's truth. (We will learn later that the Corinthians became so occupied with gifts that they all wanted to do great and miraculous things.)

The spiritual gifts of the Corinthians, and their ability to speak about the faith, served to confirm Paul's testimony about Christ to the believers at Corinth. It is Paul who was giving the testimony *about* Christ (last part of verse 6); the reference is not to Christ's giving a testimony.

(1:7-8) so that you come short in no gift, eagerly waiting for the revelation of our Lord Jesus Christ, who will confirm you to the end, that you may be blameless in the day of our Lord Jesus Christ.

The phrase "come short" translates the Greek *hystereo*. The basic meaning is "to lack." The Christians at Corinth had all the spiritual gifts they needed to live the Christian life and to witness for Christ.

The "revelation" of Jesus Christ refers to His second coming. Jesus will be manifested without the veil of humanity (as was the case at His first coming). When Jesus comes again, He will be revealed in blazing splendor. Because the Lord's return is always imminent, it was proper for the Corinthians (as it is for us) to be "eagerly waiting"[2] for His coming.

Jesus will "confirm you to the end"—meaning that He will keep on dealing with us—rebuking, pleading, admonishing, and chastening right up to the end. Through the work of Jesus on the cross, we will be "blameless." To be "blameless" is not to be "sinless"—but by the grace of God our lives will be lived so nobly that there will not be loopholes for others to *justly* latch on to and criticize. Nothing in our lives will bring shame to the cause of Christ.

---

[2] The Greek word *apekdechomenous* (eagerly waiting) means to wait with eager anticipation, but also with activity. It involves *working* while we watch and wait for the Lord's coming.

(1:9) God is faithful, by whom you were called into the fellowship of His Son, Jesus Christ our Lord.

As children of God, none of us ever needs to doubt God's grace and His goodness to us. Even in the hard places of life, God is faithful.[3] He is dependable and loyal and does keep His promises.

As Christians, we are in partnership with Jesus. We are in fellowship with Him. Our calling is to make His interests our interests. The calling is to let our minds, our bodies, and our spirits be aimed at promoting His glory. Our chief aim in life is to exalt His person, His majesty, and the greatness of His power.

2. The Exhortation to Unity (1:10-17)

The major part of the first four chapters of First Corinthians deals with the divided state of the church at Corinth. Instead of being unified in Christ, it was split into various parties of people who had attached themselves to the names of several leaders and teachers.

Divisions of various kinds have always plagued the church. *Separating* from those who continuously adhere to false and unscriptural teachings is a Christian duty; it is not necessarily a sin. However, *dividing* because of personal ambition or because of honor for certain personalities is always harmful and wrong. We need a humble spirit and a readiness to make concessions when matters come up about which the people of God disagree.

We all tend to romanticize the past and look back, wishing things now were as they had been in former times. But when we read the account of what was happening at

---

[3] The faithfulness of God and His Word is a constant theme in the Bible. It is clearly stated in Psalms 89 and 119. Also, "great is His faithfulness" (Lamentations 3:23).

Corinth, we recognize that there were some black spots in the church's past.

(1:10) Now I plead with you, brethren, by the name of our Lord Jesus Christ, that you all speak the same thing, and that there be no divisions among you, but that you be perfectly joined together in the same mind and in the same judgment.

Paul appealed to the Corinthians first of all, calling upon them to manifest a *united* testimony. In the latter part of verse 10 he added a plea for inner harmony. The Greek word translated "divisions" is *schismata* which literally means "a crack" or "a tear."

The words "perfectly joined together" are from a Greek word translated "mending" (their nets) in Matthew 4:21. The nets sagged more at some places than at others. There were knots tied at various places on the net. It did not look symmetrical, yet the net was a unit, and held many fish when dipped each time into the water. The reference in verse 10b refers to restoring, mending, or repairing that which is rent or disordered.

Division generally has to do with marginal matters. Jesus alluded to schism when He described a house divided against itself (Mark 3:25). Believers are to avoid fellowship with those who create dissension within the body of Christ (Romans 16:17). The Lord longs for unity[4] and mutual love among believers in the church. Jesus prayed for harmony among God's people (John 17:21-23). Unity is a oneness characterized by humility, love, and singleness of purpose.

---

4 *Unity* can be illustrated by a giant oak tree with branches that differ in many ways. Some of the branches are thick; others are thin. Some are long; others are short. Some are crooked; others are full of knots—but there are inner cords that bind. *Uniformity* can be illustrated by a stack of 2 x 4's, all the same length and thickness. With no inner core that binds them together, a pile of 2 x 4's can more easily be toppled than can the giant oak tree.

(1:11) For it has been declared to me concerning you, my brethren, by those of Chloe's household, that there are contentions among you.

Paul had received word about the divisions at Corinth from members of Chloe's household. Her name was evidently well known to the Corinthians.

The problem that Paul was dealing with was not something spread by gossip. Those who shared with Paul the concern about conditions at Corinth were willing to be identified. They reported that there was quarreling and bickering among the believers in the church at Corinth, and indeed such conduct should not exist among believers.

Paul's use of the term "my brethren" helps to soften the rebuke of the bad report. The source of the report was identified, and thus, if the report were not true, those of Chloe's household would have to face the fact that they were guilty of libeling the Christians at Corinth.

(1:12) Now I say this, that each of you says, "I am of Paul," or "I am of Apollos," or "I am of Cephas," or "I am of Christ."

As far as we know, the divisions in Corinth were not caused by doctrinal disputes. The Corinthian church divided over who was considered the best leader. There were four factions, each having its own preferences and its own leader. Paul and Apollos and Peter all preached the same gospel and brought the same message, but their approaches were different.

There were those who said I am of Paul. Paul was the teacher, and some said, "I like real Bible teaching." Paul may have used his name first to let the people know that it was just as wrong to claim to be followers of Paul, as it was to be followers of the other church leaders. Paul thus made it clear that he was not envious of the others.

There were some who said I am of Apollos. Apollos was an eloquent speaker. Some said, "I like a man who can stand up and preach a wonderful sermon; I want something that can chill my blood and stir my soul."

There were those who said I am of Cephas. Peter was the practical man. Peter's style was to present the message with simplicity rather than with eloquence. They liked his homely down-to-earth handling of the Word.

Others at Corinth were saying I am of Christ. They said, "You may have Peter and Paul and Apollos; we are followers of Christ; we don't want a man teaching us." This group may have been a small self-righteous sect who claimed they were the true Christians at Corinth. The real fault was not in saying that they belonged to Christ, but in acting as if Christ belonged only to them.

The difficulty at Corinth arose perhaps from perfectly legitimate likes and dislikes—but they forgot that the importance of the gospel truth lay not in the *messenger*, but in the *message*. They were polarizing around prominent church leaders. They were dividing over men instead of uniting around a message.[5]

(1:13) Is Christ divided? Was Paul crucified for you? Or were you baptized in the name of Paul?

Paul quickly dispelled the idea of distinctions such as those mentioned in verse 12. He showed the foolishness of their divisions by asking three questions with obvious negative answers: "Is Christ divided?" "Was Paul crucified

---

[5] The early Brethren were very careful about emphasizing loyalty to a man. Floyd E. Mallott says that when the Brethren were first organized, "They mutually pledged their word, that no one should ever divulge, who among them had baptized first (according to the lot), in order to cut off all occasion of calling them [the Brethren] after any man, because they had found that such foolishness had already been reproved by Paul in his writings to the Corinthians" (*Studies in Brethren History*, page 31).

for you?" "Were you baptized in Paul's name?" Readers knew that the answer to each question was *No*.

We owe a great deal to Paul. We will be able to talk with him in Heaven and tell him what his teaching has meant to us—but Paul was not crucified for us! Neither was Apollos or Peter crucified for us. And so Paul is saying, "Get your eyes off men, and fix your gaze on Jesus."

(1:14-16) I thank God that I baptized none of you except Crispus and Gaius, lest anyone should say that I had baptized in my own name. Yes, I also baptized the household of Stephanas. Besides, I do not know whether I baptized any other.

The Corinthians apparently took great pride in who performed the rite of water baptism for them. They may have boasted that baptism was worth more if done by an apostle rather than by a person of less stature. Faithful ministers of the gospel always baptize in the name of Christ—not in their own names.

The mention of baptism led Paul to make clear that baptism by him would have no special significance. Paul was glad that he was so busy preaching that he did not take much time to perform baptisms, lest people would be given the opportunity to declare that they were followers of him. Paul's opponents could not say that he was trying to establish a sect that bore his name

Paul did not say, "I am thankful that you were not baptized." Paul believed that baptism was an important rite (Galatians 3:27), but to believe that there was value in being baptized *by certain church leaders* was erroneous thinking. Paul did baptize a few persons (Crispus and Gaius and Stephanas), but those were the only ones he could think of at the moment. Because Paul had baptized so few, it was less likely that people would build a party around him.

(1:17) For Christ did not send me to baptize, but to preach the gospel, not with wisdom of words, lest the cross of Christ should be made of no effect.

Paul was primarily an evangelist, and an evangelist goes from place to place laying a foundation. Paul *does not say* that Christ sent him, telling him not to baptize; instead, he says that Christ sent him *to preach the gospel* which was his primary task. Baptism would follow his preaching, but that was apparently usually done by local overseers.

Paul's assignment was not to see how many people he could baptize, but to preach the message of the Cross. He was concerned that *the message of the cross of Christ* did not become secondary and emptied of its power.

The phrase "not with wisdom of words" indicates that it does not necessarily take a great orator to make a great preacher. Those who are lovers of oratory may court the applause of the audience, but their message, at the same time, may not lift up the central message of the gospel.

The leaders in the church were sent to preach the message of a crucified Christ. They were to faithfully proclaim the truth, and the believers were to live in harmony and in unity.[6] Instead, the brothers and sisters at Corinth had formed parties around their favorite teachers, and thus were more occupied with the messenger than with the message. Such divisions must not be counted as acceptable among believers.

---

[6] To let a consistent testimony for Christ, we must work together in unity. Think of the simple task of flying a kite: Who flew the kite? "I did," said the sticks; "I did," said the paper; "No, I did," said the boy; "No, I did," said the wind. But they all flew the kite together! If the sticks had broken, or the paper had torn, or the wind had died down—the kite would have fallen down. Each had a part to play. And so it is in the Lord's work. We each have a task to do—families to nurture and train; neighbors to visit; finances to give; classes to teach. God expects all of us to work together.

Chapter 2

THE GOSPEL AND THE INTELLECTUAL
1 Corinthians 1:18-3:4

The divisions which existed at Corinth were related primarily to the philosophy of life which the members of the church had embraced. The key word in this section of the epistle is the word "wisdom"—mentioned twenty-one times. The opposite of wisdom ("foolishness") is mentioned seven times. The phrase "with wisdom of words" (1:17) announces a new section of the letter.

1. False Wisdom and the Gospel (1:18-31)

There were several causes for the divisions at Corinth. Not only did the Christians at Corinth tend to focus on loyalty to certain of God's messengers, but they also experienced divisions among themselves *because they misunderstood God's message of the Cross.*

Paul shows in these verses that worldly wisdom (which the Corinthians prized highly), is a false wisdom—the very opposite of the wisdom of God.

(1:18) For the message of the cross is foolishness to those who are perishing, but to us who are being saved it is the power of God.

Paul explains here that the message of the cross produces two effects: 1) It is foolishness to those who are lost; 2) It is the power of God to those who are being saved.

Paul, without apology, divides humanity into two categories—the lost and the saved. *Those who are saved* see the Cross as the means by which God's salvation is made possible. *Those who are lost* see the Cross as a mark of stupidity and worthlessness.

Typical worldly wisdom is foolishness because it has no power to *change* human beings. The gospel of Jesus Christ, by way of contrast, is *the power of God* to blast the sinner out of his sins into the kingdom of God. It is powerful enough to make a liar tell the truth, and an alcoholic to put away his bottle, and a fallen woman to become a beautiful witness for the Lord.

Cicero, who lived in New Testament times, once said, "The Cross speaks of that which is so shameful and so horrible that it should never be mentioned in polite society." The Apostle Paul, however, continued to say, "But God forbid that I should glory except in the cross of our Lord Jesus Christ" (Galatians 6:14).

(1:19) For it is written: "I will destroy the wisdom of the wise, and bring to nothing the understanding of the prudent."

The "wisdom" which Paul condemns is *the desire of human beings to save themselves by their own skills*. Paul is not denying the importance of education. Many times those without a formal education are just as inclined to reject God's salvation as are those who have academic training.

The point of verse 19 is that *the Cross is the sole instrument of salvation*. The quote is from Isaiah 29:14. The rulers of Judah sought to rely on Egypt for assistance in stopping the invasion of Sennacherib, the Assyrian army officer. Relying on help from Egypt is symbolic of depending on human help to solve our problems. The quotation is given to show that God dismisses mere human wisdom as a means of achieving salvation.

In fact, God will destroy (bring to nothing) the wisdom of this world.

(1:20-21) Where is the wise? Where is the scribe? Where is the disputer of this age? Has not God made foolish

the wisdom of this world? For since, in the wisdom of God, the world through wisdom did not know God, it pleased God through the foolishness of the message preached to save those who believe.

In verse 20, "the wise" is the *thinker*, "the scribe" is the *writer*, and "the disputer" refers to the *speaker*.

The world has a wisdom all of its own, but it is limited by the forces of the darkened mind. By worldly wisdom humans are unable to come to the knowledge of God. Worldly wisdom can discover some of the secrets of nature. Worldly wisdom can construct useful devices and build magnificent structures—but all of this does not give mankind the knowledge of God.

In verse 21, Paul contrasts the preaching of the Cross with the wisdom of this world. The *act of preaching* is not foolish, but *the message preached* is considered foolish by the worldly mind. What the world calls "foolishness" God has transformed into divine wisdom.

(1:22-24) For Jews request a sign, and Greeks seek after wisdom; but we preach Christ crucified, to the Jews a stumbling block and to the Greeks foolishness, but to those who are called, both Jews and Greeks, Christ the power of God and the wisdom of God.

The Jews wanted visible signs to support a teaching (Matthew 16:4; John 4:48). The Greeks looked for a philosophic proof for a teaching (Acts 17:19-21). But the true gospel involves the preaching of a Person. The focus of Christian preaching is "Christ crucified."

To the Jews, Christ was *"a stumbling block."* Jews expected a victorious Messiah to establish a kingdom of Israel and overturn the power of Rome. The Cross refuted the whole idea that the Messiah would come and overthrow the Roman power.

To the Gentiles, the preaching of a crucified Christ was *"foolishness."* An executed criminal becomes the savior of sinners! That is foolish! How can the horrible death of an insignificant Galilean offer deliverance from the penalty of death?

To "those who are called" (that is, to "the saved"), Christ produces a change which can only be attributed to the power of God! Christ can change a swearing, lying, cheating, adulterous sinner into an honest, truth-telling, beautiful witness for the Lord. Peter, who cut off the right ear of the high priest's servant (Luke 22:50), a few weeks later preached a mighty sermon which led to the conversion of three thousand souls (Acts 2:14-41). After the Holy Spirit came in new power, Peter was a different man.

(1:25) Because the foolishness of God is wiser than men, and the weakness of God is stronger than men.

What is "the foolishness of God"? It is to declare that a man named Jesus Christ, who once lived in celestial glory with His Father, and who had part in creating the heavens and the earth—would then come down and somehow enter the womb of the Virgin Mary and be born in a stable and laid in a manger. And then, when He hung on the cross, God, in some mysterious way, put the sins of the entire world on His shoulders! And then, He was buried and three days later was alive again! To the worldly mind, that is plain foolishness!

And yet this so-called foolish and weak thing is used of God to provide the incentive for men and women to live a holy life. The true plan of salvation involves preaching a Person, not a system of human philosophy.

(1:26) For you see your calling, brethren, that not many wise according to the flesh, not many mighty, not many noble, are called.

The *wise* are the intellectuals; the *mighty* are the ruling class; the *noble* are those from the aristocratic class of society. Over the years, not many[7] persons of high birth and education have responded to the call of the gospel.

Some Christians have come from the higher ranks of society.[8] Yet it remains true that the great masses of Christians over the years have been simple and humble folk—fishermen, tax collectors, and Galilean peasants.. The masses of Christians were then, as now, from the more humble ranks of life.

The words "according to the flesh" mean "judged by human standards." In God's scale of values, ordinary and little things often take on a profound significance—the widow's mite, the cup of cold water, or simple hospitality shown to a stranger.

(1:27) But God has chosen the foolish things of the world to put to shame the wise, and God has chosen the weak things of the world to put to shame the things which are mighty;

The "foolish things" and the "weak things" are those things esteemed to be foolish and weak among humans.

God used *the tear of a baby* to move the heart of Pharaoh's daughter. He used *David's sling* to overthrow the Philistine giant. God used *a little maid* to bring the "mighty" Naaman to Elisha. He used *a widow with a handful of meal* to sustain the prophet Elijah. Jesus used *a little child* to teach His disciples a much needed lesson on

---

[7] We notice that the text says "not many"—which is not the same as if it said "not any." God has used men like Luther and Calvin and Wesley, but He also used a shoe cobbler like William Carey and a mill worker like David Livingstone to propagate the gospel message.

[8] These have included Dionysius at Athens (Acts 17:34), Sergius Paulus the proconsul of Cyprus (Acts 13:6-12), noble ladies at Thessalonica (Acts 17:4, 12), Erastus, city treasurer from Corinth (Romans 16:23), and others.

humility. God often uses weak things and lowly persons to accomplish His purposes.

God in His grace has showered His mercy on the foolish and weak of this world, and made them strong and wise in Christ. What the world usually despises, God can use; what the world calls foolishness, God often transforms into divine wisdom.

(1:28-29) and the base things of the world and the things which are despised God has chosen, and the things which are not, to bring to nothing the things that are, that no flesh should glory in His presence.

The term "base things" refers literally to those who are not of noble birth. The term "base things of the world" could well be translated "the lowly of the world"—that is, the class which included slaves and people who were sometimes despised. God speaks in this way to show those who seem to be important ("the things that are")—that they can accomplish nothing for their own salvation by their wisdom and their importance.

Not only is *the message* of the gospel foolish to the worldly mind, but God uses *weak human beings* to convey the message. He does not use many mighty or noble persons. God's purpose is to exclude all boasting about self-achievement (verse 29).

God is looking for folks who are foolish enough to believe that He is big enough to do the impossible through nothing!

(1:30-31) But of Him you are in Christ Jesus, who became for us wisdom from God—and righteousness and sanctification and redemption—that, as it is written, "He who glories, let him glory in the Lord."

God the Father has decreed that many marvelous blessings should come to those who "are in Christ Jesus."

Christ Jesus is the "wisdom from God." And God's wisdom is given to establish righteousness, and to produce sanctification and redemption.

Christ is our *righteousness*—It is by His sole merits that we are pardoned and accepted of God (see Philippians 3:8-9). His righteousness is credited to our account.

Christ is our *sanctification*—He, by the Spirit, is transforming us into His likeness "from glory to glory" (see 2 Corinthians 3:18; Hebrews 12:14).

Christ is our *redemption*—He is our Deliverer from guilt, sin, and hell (see Acts 16:15-18).

The goal of God the Father in bestowing all these things upon the believer in Christ, is that we may not claim any merit to ourselves in salvation, but that we might give God all the praise.

Salvation comes through faith in a Person (the Lord Jesus Christ), not through adhering to some weak human philosophy. Cultural and economic advantages have no part in God's plan of salvation. Every human being is bankrupt before God, and must repent and receive God's grace manifested in Jesus Christ in order to experience salvation. None of us can claim any merit in ourselves, and thus we need to give God all the praise for our redemption.

2. The Nature of Christian Preaching (2:1-5)

Paul was so convinced of the superiority of the word of the cross over the wisdom of the world, that he resolved to fervently preach the gospel message with simple and ungarnished words.

God has acted contrary to human wisdom in the way He has chosen to save people. In God's plan, a crucified criminal became the Savior. But it is not only *God's method of saving people* that is contrary to human wisdom; *the manner in which the gospel is preached* is also contrary to human wisdom.

The true character of Christian ministry is found in verse 2, where the Apostle Paul says that his determined goal was to preach only the crucified Christ as the way of salvation. His only design in going to the city of Corinth was to proclaim the message that "Christ died for our sins according to the Scriptures" (1 Corinthians 15:3)—and the message was proclaimed in an unadorned manner.

Paul's preaching was marked by human weakness and divine power. Paul came to Corinth, not presenting a message with excellence of speech, but with the simple message that Christ died on the cross for our sins.

(2:1) And I, brethren, when I came to you, did not come with excellence of speech or of wisdom declaring to you the testimony of God.

Paul remembered back to the time he first came to Corinth (described in Acts 18). He did not come with lofty words and brilliant ideas. The Greeks loved to reason, to discuss, and to debate. They were fond of rich oratory, but Paul aimed to speak the simple truth in language that was understandable to all.[9]

Paul's message was simple, but simple preaching is not shallow preaching. It requires lots of study and careful preparation, but the message is stated with clear, direct, and understandable words. Paul is not deprecating eloquence

---

[9] It is tempting for a preacher to use flowery words. For example, in answer to the question, "How much is two plus two?"—one orator said, "When in the course of human events it becomes necessary to take the numeral of the second denomination and add it to the number two, I say without any fear of successful contradiction—that the answer will invariably be four!" His verbose response used 40 words instead of one word to answer the question. The preacher must be careful to make each word count so that the presentation is not heavy with a multitude of words.

and implying that preaching should be presented in bad English—but preaching must not be based on mere human ideas nor presented with highfalutin language which is difficult for the congregation to follow.

(2:2) For I determined not to know anything among you except Jesus Christ and Him crucified.

The people of Corinth (like all other people) did not need another philosophy, nor did they need political advice. They needed Christ—and Paul resolved to preach Christ as the answer to man's basic need. The burden of his soul was to make known the message of Jesus and His death on the cross. Just as from every town and village in England, there is a road that leads to London, so from every text in Scripture there is a road to Christ.

Paul did not preach on subjects like "How to get along with your mother-in-law" or "Is the planet Mars inhabited?" Paul's preaching was Christ-centered—it focused on the fact and the meaning of the crucifixion of Jesus. It was preaching that centered on what God has done in Christ for the salvation of human beings.

(2:3) I was with you in weakness, in fear, and in much trembling.

Most preachers know something about what Paul was saying. It's not that Paul feared for his own safety, or that he was ashamed of the gospel—but he was burdened with the weight of getting his message clearly proclaimed.

The British commentator, William Barclay, once said, "The preacher who is really effective is the preacher whose heart beats faster while he waits to speak." He went on to say that if there is no fluttering, "then it is time that he stopped entering" the pulpit. The preacher who has no fear, no tension, and no anxiety—without doubt is putting too much confidence in his own abilities.

Paul was aware of the seriousness of his mission, and thus the task of preaching the true gospel in the corrupt city of Corinth was faced with great concern. He had butterflies in his stomach, not because he feared the faces of his audience, but because he wanted to be sure his message met the approval of God.

(2:4) And my speech and my preaching were not with persuasive words of human wisdom, but in demonstration of the Spirit and of power,

Paul's message was proclaimed in a very plain and simple manner. The word "speech" refers to the actual delivery, and the word "preaching" refers to the content of the message.

An older sister in Christ came out from a church service one Sunday morning with a Bible under her arm. She had been disappointed with the eloquent words used in the message. She said, "It was a dictionary, not a Bible, I should have taken with me."

The phrase "in demonstration of the Spirit and of power" means that Paul's preaching was a manifestation of more than mere human power. His preaching changed the minds and lives of people, making them different persons. It was preaching anointed with Holy Spirit power.

(2:5) that your faith should not be in the wisdom of men but in the power of God.

Our faith (if it is real saving faith) must stand firmly upon God's Word, and not on man's lofty ideas.

Imagine a system of faith built around the political power of the Roman Empire in New Testament times. Where is that Empire today? Or suppose our faith was centered on the teachings of science in the 1500s? The scientists of our era have repudiated just about everything that men taught in the 1500s. But God's truth is eternal, and

God's power to change lives *is as great now* as it was in the days of Martin Luther, John Wesley, and Alexander Mack.

3. True Wisdom and the Spirit (2:6—3:4)

Human wisdom is characterized by the desire to live independently of God. It is centered upon life on earth, and is marked by rebellion against God. Yet the church is not without wisdom. To those who are called—*Christ the true wisdom of God* is made our wisdom (1:30)—and is increasingly comprehended as maturity develops.

This true wisdom was hidden in past ages, and was not recognized by worldly men—but it is now revealed through the Spirit.

The wisdom that Paul proclaims centers on the preaching of the cross, a description of the manner by which God saves individuals.

(2:6-7) However, we speak wisdom among those who are mature, yet not the wisdom of this age, nor of the rulers of this age, who are coming to nothing. But we speak the wisdom of God in a mystery, the hidden wisdom which God ordained before the ages for our glory,

In order to avoid the charge that he is depreciating reason and glorifying ignorance—Paul says that *we do speak words of great wisdom*, but not the wisdom of the world, rather the wisdom of God.

The "wisdom of this age" promotes the idea of trying to get more and more material things; it seeks to become aggressive and to stand up for one's rights; it speaks about ending wars between nations, but has no remedy for the war that keeps on raging in the human heart. It cannot solve the world's problems.

The "wisdom of God in a mystery" is a New Testament truth not previously revealed, but made known to believers by the apostles and prophets in the early church age. The mystery of the gospel includes the great truth that now Jews and Gentiles are made one in Christ.

(2:8) which none of the rulers of this age knew; for had they known, they would not have crucified the Lord of glory.

The "wisdom" spoken by Paul was not understood by the great men of the world—the political figures, the military men, the financiers and philosophers and scientists. Civil rulers such as Pilate and Herod (who condemned Jesus) didn't know (or were unwilling to believe) that the Man who stood before them in Pilate's judgment hall—was God, manifested in flesh.

God's wisdom is not the same as ordinary human wisdom. If worldly wisdom had given those rulers the ability to understand Jesus, they would not have crucified Him. They failed to realize that the "criminal" on the cross was actually the Lord of glory. The title "Lord of glory" is likely the most exalted title one can ever attribute to Christ. It is clear evidence that Jesus Christ is equal in dignity and majesty with God the Father.

(2:9) But as it is written: "Eye has not seen, nor ear heard, nor have entered into the heart of man the things which God has prepared for those who love Him."

The "things which God has prepared for those who love Him" are not *fully* visible to us while we are here in this life—but we can be sure that God has prepared some wonderful things for His people. These include not only the glories of Heaven, but also the pardon of our sins, the redemption of our bodies, peace on earth, and eternal fellowship with God.

No matter how brilliant one may be—mere man cannot understand the simple truths of the gospel, nor can he comprehend all that God has in store for him in the future. Human eyes and human ears and human hearts (apart from God's revelation) cannot fathom it all.

(2:10) But God has revealed them to us through His Spirit. For the Spirit searches all things, yes, the deep things of God.

The simple, uneducated, and untrained Christian (who may barely be able to read or write), under the Holy Spirit's direction, can often benefit from a Bible passage which a highly learned person *without the Spirit* cannot comprehend.[10]

The Greek word translated *searches* means "to carefully investigate so as to fully understand." The Spirit fully understands all things—the deep things that are hidden in the counsels and purposes of God. The Spirit understands concepts like the purpose of suffering, the destiny of those who never heard the gospel, etc.

(2:11) For what man knows the things of a man except the spirit of the man which is in him? Even so no one knows the things of God except the Spirit of God.

Only *we* know our own thoughts. This is not to deny the fact that *God* knows us better. No one can really know what others are thinking, except those individuals themselves. And in order to understand others, we must have "the spirit of the man." An *animal* cannot understand our thinking. Just so, the only One who can understand the things of God is "the Spirit of God."

---

[10] Our Anabaptist forefathers believed in carefully exercising spiritual discernment. Leonhard Schiemer was an Anabaptist believer imprisoned for his faith. He appealed to his fellow Christians to recognize the wiles of the devil, and to pray that "we may be preserved *through spiritual judgment (1 Cor. 2:9-10)*, not to lightly despise anyone, and thus let [no one] turn us from the faith, hope, and love which is in Christ Jesus" (page 216, *Spiritual Life in Anabaptism*, Cornelius J. Dyck).

(2:12) Now we have received, not the spirit of the world, but the Spirit who is from God, that we might know the things that have been freely given to us by God.

The "we" refers especially to the writers of the New Testament. The "spirit of the world" refers to the intellectual climate of the non-Christian world—greed, force, selfishness, ambition, and pleasure. Apart from "the Spirit who is from God," the writers could never have received the great truths revealed in Scripture. Verse 12 describes the process of God's *revelation* to humans.

The truths of God can be understood only through the Holy Spirit. The Spirit, Whom believers receive when born again, probes the depths of God. He knows what is in God, just as our spirit knows what is in us.

(2:13) These things we also speak, not in words which man's wisdom teaches but which the Holy Spirit teaches, comparing spiritual things with spiritual.

The Bible writers conveyed God's revelation about who He is, and what constitutes salvation, by using "words" which the Holy Spirit taught them to use. When the Scriptures were recorded in the original documents, the Spirit guided *the choice of words* which the writers used. Verse 13 refers especially to *the verbal inspiration* of the Scriptures.

The phrase "comparing spiritual things with spiritual" refers to the fact that spiritual truths in one part of the Bible should be compared with the truths in other parts of the Bible. We should compare and catalog spiritual truth from all parts of the Bible to make a complete and logical system of spiritual truth.

(2:14) But the natural man does not receive the things of the Spirit of God, for they are foolishness to him; nor can he know them, because they are spiritually discerned.

The "natural man"[11] is a reference to those persons who live as though there is nothing beyond this present physical life. They do not necessarily *blaspheme* God; they simply *dismiss* Him. They are secularists, without devotion to God, and blinded to spiritual matters. Unless one is born of the Spirit and taught by Him, God's revelation of truth seems meaningless and foolish.

The *natural man* lacks spiritual discernment. To him the things of the Spirit just do not make sense. By contrast, the *spiritual man* can make mature judgments because he has the mind of Christ.

The phrase "nor can he know them" indicates that those who are in "the natural man" category are totally blind to spiritual truth, no matter how cultured, sophisticated, or educated they might be. The only avenue of entrance into spiritual things is closed to them, for those things "are spiritually discerned"—and they do not have the Spirit living within. Their aims and goals are centered primarily on the things of this life.

(2:15) But he who is spiritual judges all things, yet he himself is rightly judged by no one.

The person "who is spiritual" is not necessarily one who can pray the loudest or the longest or the nicest—*but one in whom the Holy Spirit has taken over*. Such persons can discern the wonderful truths of God's Word. They can see the difference between what is of man and what is of God. They can evaluate others and can understand the trends of the age in which we live. They may never have been off to college, yet they can comprehend the deep mysteries of God.

---

[11] The Greek word *psuchikos* means "of the senses"—following one's own affections and desires. How often have we heard someone say: "Do you know what she said about me? It's only natural that I should be angry."

On the other hand, the man of the world cannot understand Him at all. Spirit-led persons cannot be "rightly judged" by those who are unconverted, for they have a distorted sense of judgment.

(2:16) For "who has known the mind of the Lord that he may instruct Him?" But we have the mind of Christ.

The words, "we have the mind of Christ," do not mean that we know all that Christ knows. The newly born child of God, however, seeks to walk in such intimate communion with Christ, that he more and more, in faith, sees things through His eyes.

Only those who have "the mind of Christ" can come close to understanding the deep truths of God. Those who are "spiritual" are enlightened by the Holy Spirit to the point where they share God's thoughts and understand God's will. The success of the gospel does not depend on human wisdom, but on God's power

(3:1) And I, brethren, could not speak to you as to spiritual people but as to carnal, as to babes in Christ.

Paul points out in the next few verses another cause for the divisions which existed among the Corinthian believers. Their lives were marked by rampant carnality, which limited their comprehension of God's wisdom.

When the Apostle Paul came to Corinth he had proclaimed the necessity of faith in Jesus Christ as the means of salvation. He preached "Jesus Christ and Him crucified" (1 Corinthians 2:2). But faith in Christ carries with it the concept of being committed to *following* Christ in daily life. The Christians at Corinth had fallen far short of that goal. Paul begins at this point to deal with their failures and some of the reasons why they had failed.

Paul found that the Corinthian believers, especially those who had just been won for Christ, were babes. They were very immature. They were labeled as "carnal." They lacked humility and mutual forbearance.

The word "carnal" (Greek, *sarkinos*, which means "fleshly") is what a person (in the natural state) cannot help being—but for the believer, the carnal state is to be subordinated to the higher law of the Spirit.

Those who were called "carnal" were professing Christians, but they were still letting the old fleshly nature control their lives. They were under the control of the "self nature" instead of being governed by the Spirit of God. They were not mature in the Christian faith.

(3:2) I fed you with milk and not with solid food; for until now you were not able to receive it, and even now you are still not able;

The believers at Corinth should have made progress by this time. It was all very well for the Corinthians to be babes when they actually were newly born, but they should have outgrown that stage long ago.

Baby Christians sometimes live as people of the flesh (*sarkinos*), desiring to please themselves. Paul typically uses the word "flesh" to refer to man's sinful nature as opposed to the higher nature. New believers occasionally are not fully yielded to Christ as Lord and do not walk in close fellowship with God. Their lives do not reflect the fruit of the Spirit (Galatians 5:22-23).

The goal for each newly born person is to grow and mature in the graces of our Lord Jesus Christ.

(3:3) for you are still carnal. For where there are envy, strife, and divisions among you, are you not carnal and behaving like mere men?

The carnal members at Corinth avoided the gross sins of intemperance, adultery, and theft—but they were envious of others and jealous of their success. They had a controversial, bitter spirit. They tended to separate from others who did not see their point of view in every detail.

Envy and strife are characteristics of carnality. Here are persons who have believed, repented, and have been baptized—but as one gets more intimately acquainted with them, he finds they are very selfish persons. They are delightful to get along with as long as they can have their own way! These are symptoms of carnality.[12] They are people who just have not grown up spiritually. They are still babies. Such attitudes do not demonstrate the true wisdom of God.

(3:4) For when one says, "I am of Paul," and another, "I am of Apollos," are you not carnal?

Paul uses his own name in this rebuke to show that it is just as wrong to follow after him as to follow after any of the other spokesmen for Christ. This party spirit is an example of human carnality. It is thinking purely on a human level and gives evidence of a lack of spiritual discernment. The true wisdom of God, by way of contrast, exalts *Christ* by living above the human-centered standards of the world.

We began this chapter on 1 Corinthians 1:18—3:4 by saying that the believers at Corinth experienced divisions not only because they favored one leader over another, but also because they misunderstood God's message of the cross. They embraced worldly wisdom rather than the wisdom of God.

---

[12] The Anabaptists were ardent foes of self-centered carnality. Pieter Pietersz (in his treatise, *The Way to the City of Peace*) says, "There is no worse cancer in the world than strife, quarreling, disunity, and envy arising through the evil work of the devil." He quotes 1 Corinthians 3:3 to state that "It is necessary therefore that we watch carefully over all those things which bring strife and disunity, that they may find no place in our hearts" (quoted in Cornelius Dyck, *Spiritual Life in Anabaptism*, pages 235 and 278).

The core of Paul's message is that believing in the crucifixion and resurrection of Jesus Christ is the only way to salvation and Heaven. God's wisdom calls for humble submission to the Lord Jesus Christ, an action which will bring fulfillment in this life and will bring the promise of everlasting life in the next world.

Marcus Whitman was a pioneer missionary to the American Indians in Oregon. He preached the message of the cross, along with all that it implies about the sinfulness of the human family. Whenever he proclaimed that message, some would protest, and ask him to give them (in their words) "good talk." "Tell us," they said, "that we are good men, brave men—and not that we are sinners."

Such resentment of the message of the cross was apparently one of the problems among the more intellectual people of Corinth. It is typical of worldly wisdom today.

Chapter 3

THE ROLE OF FAITHFUL MINISTERS
1 Corinthians 3:5—4:21

Paul continues now to speak more specifically to the concern that was expressed already in the first chapter of the letter—cautioning the Corinthians about divisions. The point in this section of the epistle is this: Why divide over preachers? They are merely servants of God (3:5-6); they are persons equal in rank (3:7-9); they are accountable to God (3:10-23).

1. The Apostles are Co-workers with God (3:5-23)

Ministers are preachers of the good news and are servants of God, not masters of people. They are intended to be agents of God, not objects of faith in which the congregation should trust.

(3:5) Who then is Paul, and who is Apollos, but ministers through whom you believed, as the Lord gave to each one?

The Greek word translated *ministers* is "diakonoi." It is the word from which we get the term "deacon." However, here it does not refer to a certain rank within the church, but rather to a servant in general. It speaks of one who is a menial worker of any sort, and who ministers under the authority of another.

We should appreciate those who minister the Word—those who serve in leadership roles in the church, but we must not set preachers on pedestals. They are merely co-workers with God; the real work is done by the Lord. It is a mistake to honor preachers instead of praising the God who enables His servants.

(3:6-7) I planted, Apollos watered, but God gave the increase. So then neither he who plants is anything, nor he who waters, but God who gives the increase.

It seems that the factions which had developed in Corinth may have been related to the variety of tasks that Paul and Apollos were expected to do there. Paul was the missionary pioneer who had been the founder of the church in Corinth. Apollos was given the duty of helping the believers to grow stronger in the faith. Paul founded the church at Corinth; Apollos had built upon the foundation established by Paul.

Paul is now explaining that many at Corinth were putting their loyalties at the wrong place. Paul had planted the seed; Apollos had watered it; but it was God who made the seed grow. Compared to God's work in making the seed grow, the one who did the planting and the one who did the watering were not really all that important. One person may plant a seed and another may water it, but neither can claim to have made the seed grow. The servant is nothing;[13] God is everything.

And so there is no room for pride on the part of those who are leaders, nor is there any benefit on the part of the members of Christ's body in developing loyalties toward certain leaders.

(3:8-9) Now he who plants and he who waters are one, and each one will receive his own reward according to his own labor. For we are God's fellow workers; you are God's field, you are God's building.

Paul refutes any idea that he and Apollos are at variance with each other. They are preaching the same gospel message, but they use different approaches. One worker leads a soul to Christ; another worker builds up the

---

[13] In light of the servant-nature of the Christian ministry, it does not seem proper to introduce visiting preachers as "one of the outstanding pastors in America," or "one who has preached in all the capitals of Europe," or "one of the greatest speakers of our times." Also, we note that using the title *reverend* was frowned upon by the Brethren already at Annual Meeting in 1867.

souls of those who are won to Christ. Workers in God's vineyard will receive fair rewards for their labors.

The preachers are "God's fellow workers." Those who preach are actually God's messenger boys. They simply do what He tells them to do.

(3:10) According to the grace of God which was given to me, as a wise master builder I have laid the foundation, and another builds on it. But let each one take heed how he builds on it.

Paul likens himself to a "master builder" (Greek, *architekton*). He proclaimed the message which declares that salvation is through Jesus alone, and thus by God's grace, Paul laid the foundation.

Every Christian mother is a wise master builder (the architect) of a young life; she is a minister of God when she molds that life according to the pattern of God's Word.

We are to be careful how we build—and thus it is a solemn thing to be a Bible teacher in a local congregation, and to be a parent of children in our families.

(3:11) For no other foundation can anyone lay than that which is laid, which is Jesus Christ.

Paul does not want to give the impression that good works, church tradition, humanism, and science etc., are acceptable foundations for the church. Once the foundation is laid, it does not need to be repeated. The foundation of the church is Jesus Christ, including His person and work on the cross. There are no other admissible foundations.

(3:12-13) Now if anyone builds on this foundation with gold, silver, precious stones, wood, hay, straw, each one's work will become clear; for the Day will declare it, because it will be revealed by fire; and the fire will test each one's work, of what sort it is.

Some teaching in the church *is helpful and lasting*, and can be likened to gold and silver and precious stones.

Precious stones are costly; only a small amount of them is of great value. At the same time, some teaching in the church *is of little value* for the spiritual lives of the members. Such teaching can be likened to wood, hay, and straw. These entities are bulky and are relatively worthless.

Verses 12-13 are often used in a general way to refer to the lives of all Christians—and it is true that all of us are building day by day—and the results of our work will be manifested at the future day of judgment. However, the context of these verses indicates that they refer *not primarily to all believers, but to pastors and teachers* who are building on the foundation referred to in verse 11.

At the time of judgment, "each one's work will become clear"—that is, the Lord will review all the labors of His servants. The review will be somewhat like the action of fire. *Service which brought glory to God and blessing to the church*—will be like gold and silver and precious stones. On the other hand, *teaching which failed to carefully instruct and edify* the congregation will be consumed.

(3:14-15) If anyone's work which he has built on it endures, he will receive a reward. If anyone's work is burned, he will suffer loss; but he himself will be saved, yet so as through fire.

There are different motives that lie behind the work of God's servants. Those whose work has edified God's people will receive a reward. Those who were engaged in mere self-exalting and useless activity will "suffer loss," yet they themselves will experience salvation, "yet so as through fire."

The passage in verses 11-15 is speaking about preachers (see verses 5-9), and the fruits of their ministries. The labors of the faithful man of God will be rewarded far beyond the reward of those who preach out of self-interest and merely in the energy of the flesh.

The words back in verse 13 ("of what sort it is") imply that it is the character of our work that counts. The reference is to *the motives that lie behind our work* for the Lord. All preachers and teachers of the Word need to take heed how they build! Those efforts which fail to bring people into a living and growing fellowship with God will not stand in that day when our service is subjected to the fire of God's judgment.

(3:16) Do you not know that you are the temple of God and that the Spirit of God dwells in you?

Every individual believer is a "temple of God." The human heart—and not the church auditorium where the people of God assemble—is the sanctuary, the place where God dwells. Paul, in this passage, however, is looking at the church as a collective company,[14] and calls upon all of us (including church leaders) to realize the holy dignity to which we are called as the dwelling place of the Spirit.

(3:17) If anyone defiles the temple of God, God will destroy him. For the temple of God is holy, which temple you are.

This passage continues to speak about preachers and the fruits of their ministries. The labors of faithful servants of God (those who "plant" and those who "water") will be rewarded far beyond the rewards of those whose messages do not edify and nurture the church.

The "gold, silver, precious stones" (3:12a) are the labors of those faithful men who proclaim the truth. The "wood, hay, [and] straw" (3:12b) are the labors of self-

---

[14] In the original Greek, the "you" (in verse 16) is plural, and thus the local church is meant. In chapter 6:19, the "you" is singular, and the reference is to each person as an individual.

aggrandizing men—those who baptize people to boost their egos, to increase the church roll, or to get bigger offerings. Those goals tend to "defile" the body of Christ.

(3:18) Let no one deceive himself. If anyone among you seems to be wise in this age, let him become a fool that he may become wise.

The words "Let no one deceive himself" are addressed to those leaders who preach from wrong motives, and thus harm the church. Paul warns them against putting on a pretense of wisdom. Instead, Paul says, "Let him become a fool" meaning that it is important to accept God's wisdom, which the world regards as folly.

(3:19-20) For the wisdom of this world is foolishness with God. For it is written, "He catches the wise in their own craftiness"; and again, "The Lord knows the thoughts of the wise, that they are futile."

For example, when the enemies of our Lord in their human wisdom, guarded the tomb of Jesus (Matthew 27:64-66), they only *made more intense* the proof of Christ's resurrection. Such wisdom is foolishness with God.

Paul knew that the Corinthians idolized those who excelled in worldly wisdom. But worldly wisdom is hollow and empty.

(3:21-23) Therefore let no one boast in men. For all things are yours: whether Paul or Apollos or Cephas, or the world or life or death, or things present or things to come— all are yours. And you are Christ's, and Christ is God's.

The phrase "let no one boast in men" is addressed to the members of the church. Do not glory in any one leader. All of them belong to God's people, and the church in turn belongs to Christ.

These last words of 1 Corinthians 3 describe the wealth which the church had in its teachers and preachers. There was a plurality of ministers who served at Corinth, and this was a great blessing, along with all the other good things in life which they had experienced.

All the riches of God are ours. We are told that *life* and even *death* are gifts from God which belong to us. Can you imagine living *forever* in the pitiful existence such as we have here on earth? The riches we enjoy here in this life are only a foretaste of the riches which are still to come.

We must learn to appreciate the gifts that are given to us. If we are children of God, then we are joint-heirs with Christ, and some day we shall be glorified and live together with other transformed believers and with the Lord Jesus (Romans 8:17). What a wonderful gift!

There is a legitimate appreciation one should have for those who proclaim the Word as ministers of the gospel, but it is highly inconsistent for God's people to pit one preacher against another and divide over the personalities and the gifts of those who deliver God's messages to us.

The appeal given already in chapter 1, verses 10-17, has been carried through the early chapters of First Corinthians. We are to strive for maintaining the unity of the faith, and not waste our energies engaging in hurtful divisions.

2. An Evaluation of God's Ministers (4:1-5)

The focus in 1 Corinthians 4 is upon those who are called to preach the gospel and to instruct the church in the ways of God. The question presented in these verses is: "How shall churches look at the ministers of the gospel?"

(4:1) Let a man so consider us, as servants of Christ and stewards of the mysteries of God.

The word *servants* literally means "those who are subordinate to authorities." This does not mean that the local church is to "lord it over" those who are called to preach, but refers to the fact that the "servants" are those who labor under the authority of Christ.

Stewards are those who care for and manage the person or the property of another. Stewards of "the mysteries of God" are those who proclaim and teach the revelation which God has given in the Scriptures.

(4:2) Moreover it is required in stewards that one be found faithful.

The steward manages, but he does not own. Ministers are not to proclaim their own ideas or to lift up their own dreams. Instead, they are to *faithfully* teach the Word of God. It is much more important to be faithful than it is to be popular. The word "faithful" means to be loyal and supportive. The minister is not to depart from the obvious meaning of the Scriptures.

(4:3) But with me it is a very small thing that I should be judged by you or by a human court. In fact, I do not even judge myself.

For Paul, it was "a very small thing" to be judged by the Corinthians. He was determined not to let a little bit of criticism from the people crush him, nor a little bit of praise puff him up. In fact, he was not willing to trust his own judgment. Paul was aware that our own self-centered natures are biased in favor of ourselves, and so he was not willing to make a judgment about his ministry.

(4:4) For I know of nothing against myself, yet I am not justified by this; but He who judges me is the Lord.

Paul was not aware of any charge of unfaithfulness against him, but even if he is not conscious of any charge against himself—he is not justified by this.

Even though Paul may think himself to be without known fault—that does not make it so and acquit him of any wrongdoing. All of us are inclined to build ourselves up in our own minds. God sees the heart and the inner thoughts and motivations that may be unrealized by us.

He who "judges me is the Lord." The day will come when all hidden things will be brought to light, and the purposes of our hearts will be revealed.

(4:5) Therefore judge nothing before the time, until the Lord comes, who will both bring to light the hidden things of darkness and reveal the counsels of the hearts. Then each one's praise will come from God.

When the Lord Jesus returns and the judgment takes place, then every person will receive God's verdict—and will either receive commendation or disapproval.

We can hear what comes from the lips and we can note outward actions, but we do not know all the hidden springs behind human conduct. The final "praise" (Greek, "appraisal") will come from God. The Lord, who knows the hearts of humans, will give the final evaluation. Therefore, all fault-finding, negative criticism, gossip, and judging by limited human beings must stop!

3. The Low Estate of God's Ministers (4:6-13)

The Corinthians seemed to be puffed up in favor of one minister over another. But the apostles, who were the subjects of their pride in certain church leaders, were mere human beings who lived lowly lives, often working hard with their hands to meet their needs.

(4:6) Now these things, brethren, I have figuratively transferred to myself and Apollos for your sakes, that you may learn in us not to think beyond what is written, that none of you may be puffed up on behalf of one against the other.

The Corinthian believers were forming parties around a number of teachers, but out of courtesy, Paul names only Apollos and himself. He did not mention the names of others. Paul is saying that God's people should not take pride in some leaders and despise others—and that includes Apollos and me!

The people at Corinth were carried away in their admiration for certain leaders, even to the point that they tended *to listen to them* above what is written in God's Word. Paul is admonishing the young Christians by saying, "Don't divide over these men; instead, unite around what is written in the Scriptures."

(4:7) For who makes you differ from another? And what do you have that you did not receive? Now if you did indeed receive it, why do you glory as if you had not received it?

There is no reason for any servant of Christ to exalt himself above another. If some Christian teachers are more gifted than others, it is only because God made them so. Everything they have was received from the Lord—and so, why be proud and puffed up?

(4:8) You are already full! You are already rich! You have reigned as kings without us—and indeed I could wish you did reign, that we also might reign with you!

With a note of sarcasm, Paul accused the believers at Corinth of behaving as if they had already become kings. Christians someday expect to reign with Christ, but these folks acted as if they had already reached this point. They behaved as if they had no flaws and no further need to grow. Paul wished that this were true, for if it were, then he and the other apostles would be kings with them.

(4:9) For I think that God has displayed us, the apostles, last, as men condemned to death; for we have been made a spectacle to the world, both to angels and to men.

In contrast to the self-satisfaction and pride of the Corinthians, Paul symbolically pictured the apostles as thrown into an arena with wild animals.

The words "we have been made a spectacle to the world" allude to the gladiators who performed in the amphitheater. Men who were condemned for some crime, were often tortured and exposed to the wild animals in the coliseum. Their blood and agonies became the source of entertainment for a whole population of spectators.

The word "spectacle" is translated from the Greek *theatron*—meaning "a show," something displayed on a screen. The apostles were sometimes ridiculed, beaten, mocked, and treated like criminals.

(4:10-13) We are fools for Christ's sake, but you are wise in Christ! We are weak, but you are strong! You are distinguished, but we are dishonored! To the present hour we both hunger and thirst, and we are poorly clothed, and beaten, and homeless. And we labor, working with our own hands. Being reviled, we bless; being persecuted, we endure; being defamed, we entreat. We have been made as the filth of the world, the offscouring of all things until now.

The people at Corinth were enjoying the security and the plenty of their favored places, while the apostles were without sufficient food and decent clothing,[15] and were the objects of mob violence[16] and without permanent homes. While the apostles were enduring such hardships, the Christians at Corinth were indulging in childish jealousies and carnal rivalries.

The apostles were like gladiators, in a fight with Satan's kingdom. The members of the church at Corinth were like spectators—sitting at ease and watching the struggle from a safe distance.

---

[15] See 2 Corinthians 11:27 "with labour and toil, with many a sleepless night, in hunger and thirst, in frequent fastings, in cold, and with insufficient clothing" (Weymouth).

[16] For example, in Acts 23:2 we read, "And the high priest Ananias commanded those who stood by him to strike him on the mouth."

4. The Concern of God's Ministers (4:14-21)

In these verses, Paul gives a final admonition to the believers on the subject of dividing over church leaders.

(4:14) I do not write these things to shame you, but as my beloved children I warn you.

Paul was not speaking in bitterness with the idea of humiliating the believers. He had a genuine interest in the welfare of the church (his "beloved children"), and so he concluded with a concerned warning. The word "warn" (Greek, *noutheto*) means "to admonish" or "to advise" the Corinthians of the seriousness of their actions.

(4:15-16) For though you might have ten thousand instructors in Christ, yet you do not have many fathers; for in Christ Jesus I have begotten you through the gospel. Therefore I urge you, imitate me.

The Apostle Paul was the spiritual father of the Christians at Corinth. He was the one who led them to the Lord, and even though other teachers would come along, they would not have the same personal interest in the saints as that which a father provides for his own children.

Paul urged his readers to imitate him, just as children are generally instructed to follow the example of their fathers. A man must practice what he preaches in order to speak like that.

(4:17) For this reason I have sent Timothy to you, who is my beloved and faithful son in the Lord, who will remind you of my ways in Christ, as I teach everywhere in every church.

As an expression of his fatherly love, Paul planned to send Timothy[17] to Corinth—perhaps along with this

---

[17] In 1 Thessalonians 3:1-3 Timothy is called "our brother and minister of God, and our fellow laborer in the gospel of Christ." Here in 1 Corinthians 4 he is called "my beloved and faithful son in the Lord." That description would be a remarkable epitaph on a tombstone.

letter he was writing. Paul loved Timothy as a dear son, and trusted him in the work of ministry.

Paul was consistent in his teaching. He practiced what he preached. Timothy would tell the people in the church at Corinth more about Paul's conduct and his teaching. To "teach" the Word is to tell and explain its truths. Paul was careful to present the same teaching in each congregation where he had gone..

(4:18-21) Now some are puffed up, as though I were not coming to you. But I will come to you shortly, if the Lord wills, and I will know, not the word of those who are puffed up, but the power. For the kingdom of God is not in word but in power. What do you want? Shall I come to you with a rod, or in love and a spirit of gentleness?

Paul was planning to visit the Christians at Corinth very soon "if the Lord wills,"[18] and he wanted very much that his visit might be in love and in meekness—not marred by a need to give the church a spanking. He was concerned that some of his readers had become arrogant, and boasted that Paul would never return to the church at Corinth.

If the Corinthians continued to follow human pride by dividing into factions over church leaders, Paul would rebuke them sharply upon his arrival. If they recommitted themselves to true humility based on scriptural principles, he would come in a spirit of gentleness.

---

[18] It is foolish and wicked to make plans for the future without reference to God. We can make plans, but those plans will be carried out only if the Lord wills it. The phrase "If the Lord wills" is one that we should always be saying in our hearts, and sometimes it should be uttered with our lips.

Chapter 4

MAINTAINING CHURCH DISCIPLINE
1 Corinthians 5:1-13

First Corinthians 5 deals with one of the root causes of the trouble in the church at Corinth. There were people in the church who were living immorally, and the congregation did nothing about it. Most of us know that if the conduct of members of the church is wholesome and upright, the task of persuading the world to embrace the Christian faith is not nearly as difficult.

Discipline is of several types. There is a *formative* discipline, which means "to train" and "to instruct." The church is a school where Christians are to be taught in a systematic way the "all things" which our Lord Jesus commanded. There is also a *corrective* discipline, which refers to disciplinary action that needs to be taken toward persons who violate acceptable standards of behavior. The mandates here refer to the latter type of discipline.

A careful study of the Scriptures indicates that the church not only has the obligation to proclaim the Word of God, but it also has the responsibility of restricting membership to those whose lives indicate that they are earnestly seeking to obey the Word. The Bible speaks about maintaining discipline within the Body.

1. The Occasion for Church Discipline (5:1-3)

There are a number of reasons why members of the congregation sometimes need to be disciplined. In First Corinthians 5, the offense was shocking and immoral conduct. In Romans 16:17, the offense was related to those who displayed a contentious and defiant spirit. In Titus 3:9, we read about those who get involved with "strivings about the law"—people who are dedicated to teaching error.[19] And in Matthew 18:15-18, the concern is for those who hold an irreconcilable spirit toward another Christian.

The one major example of sexual immorality mentioned in 1 Corinthians 5 was commonly known by the members of the church at Corinth. The misdemeanor was not merely a matter of suspicion and gossip. This was a case of rank sexual immorality in the church.

(5:1) It is actually reported that there is sexual immorality among you, and such sexual immorality as is not even named among the Gentiles—that a man has his father's wife!

The term "father's wife" is the Greek form of the Hebrew word for "stepmother." The word "wife" (*gunaika*) means literally "woman"—and indicates that it was the man's stepmother who was involved in the relationship. Perhaps there was not a formal marriage, but most certainly there was a permanent alliance. The phrase "to have a woman" (in the New Testament) meant "to marry her."[20]

The woman herself must have been a pagan woman, for Paul did not seek to deal with her at all.

This man had formed an illicit association with his own step-mother, a thing which would even cause revolt in the minds even of heathen people.

---

[19] In such cases the church is admonished to reject a divisive person after the first and second admonition (Titus 3:10). When Elder John Hamme (from North Carolina), in 1794, was teaching universalism (the belief that in the end all persons would be saved), he was eventually excommunicated from the church. The Annual Meeting in 1800 decided to "renounce all fellowship with each and all persons [who] hold such doctrines and views" (*The Brethren in Colonial America*, Donald Durnbaugh, page 333).

[20] See Matthew 14:4 where John the Baptist told Herod Antipas that it was not right for him "to have" his brother's wife. Herod had seduced the wife of his own brother and had married her.

(5:2) And you are puffed up, and have not rather mourned, that he who has done this deed might be taken away from among you.

Paul was shocked at the nature of the sin itself, but he was even more shocked at the attitude of the church. It seemed not to be aware that such conduct was even a problem. Even if the people in the church felt they did not know how to handle a situation like this, they could have been down before God on its knees—with breaking hearts asking that He undertake for them. Instead, the people seem to have been proud of their spirit of tolerance.

The man may have been rich and influential and formally educated. Some may have been so glad to have him as a member of the congregation that they were willing to condone his sin! The testimony of the church at Corinth was muted because it was tolerating sin in its midst. The church had complacently accepted the situation and had done nothing about it. An easy-going attitude toward sinful living is always dangerous.

(5:3) For I indeed, as absent in body but present in spirit, have already judged (as though I were present) him who has so done this deed.

Paul had fully made up his mind that this offender must be removed from the fellowship. The man must be excommunicated from the church. Paul was not about to let the congregation get "off the hook" easily regarding their responsibility in the matter.

Paul indicated that he was with the church at Corinth *in spirit*, and he had already made up his mind about what needed to be done in this case. The word "already" indicates finality in his decision. Paul was calling on the church to acknowledge the seriousness of the sin, and to begin the process of appropriate discipline.

2. The Necessity for Church Discipline (5:4-8)

Some insist on not excommunicating those who keep on engaging in grievous sins. They say we must not be too hard on them—and that instead of disfellowshipping such persons, we should throw our arms around them and sympathize with them. The Bible instructs otherwise.

(5:4-5) In the name of our Lord Jesus Christ, when you are gathered together, along with my spirit, with the power of our Lord Jesus Christ, deliver such a one to Satan for the destruction of the flesh, that his spirit may be saved in the day of the Lord Jesus.

The case before the church at Corinth was not a personal grievance, and so the group must act as a whole. They are to "gather together" (as a group) in the name of our Lord Jesus Christ and make a decision. They were to gather "in the name of our Lord," for it would be impossible to handle this case in their own wisdom.

The offending individual is to be delivered "to Satan for the destruction of the flesh." That is, the local church was to put the offending man outside the church, in the world, where Satan rules. The purpose was not to punish, but to awaken—"that his spirit may be saved in the day of the Lord Jesus."

(5:6) Your glorying is not good. Do you not know that a little leaven leavens the whole lump?

Chefs and cooks know the nature of leaven when added to the bread mixture. They add a little leaven to the dough, and the leaven will cause the dough to rise to double its original size.

Just so, if the church allows one wicked person to go unrebuked, and not dealt with after the wickedness has become known, evil conduct will spread like an infection working toward the ruin of others.

(5:7) Therefore purge out the old leaven, that you may be a new lump, since you truly are unleavened. For indeed Christ, our Passover, was sacrificed for us.

If the church at Corinth kept the offender within the fold, it was retaining the bad influence, which without doubt would spread and infect others. Leaven was sour dough—corruption in action.

The "old leaven" likely refers to the sin of being puffed up about the whole affair. In Old Testament times, on the day before the Passover, the law said that the Jew must light a candle and search the house for leaven, so that every tiny bit was cleaned out. God is concerned that the church be kept clean.[21] To shut our eyes to sin is not always a *kind* thing to do; it may be a *damaging* thing to do.

The Passover lamb was a symbolic picture of Christ our Passover, Who was sacrificed for us to bring about deliverance from sin.

(5:8) Therefore let us keep the feast, not with old leaven, nor with the leaven of malice and wickedness, but with the unleavened bread of sincerity and truth.

This is not a command for us to keep the Jewish Passover, but it is a symbolic way of picturing what Christ is to believers today. Our old life was characterized by "malice and wickedness;" the aim of the new life in Christ is to manifest "sincerity and truth."

Sincerity speaks of "purity of mind" (as opposed to the malice [ill will] of the old life). *Truth* refers to living in harmony with all of God's precepts as found in the Bible (in contrast to the evil ways of the old life). It is unthinkable

---

[21] Wilbur Stover, the pioneer Brethren missionary to India, stated in a tract that one of the reasons he loves the Church of the Brethren is "because, though she would have all men saved, she believes that it is more fitting that the kingdom of heaven be clean than crowded" (Tract #101, *Brethren Tracts and Pamphlets,* Brethren Publishing House, 1900).

for a believer to claim Christ as Savior from sin and at the same time go on living in sin.

3. The Grounds for Church Discipline (5:9-11)

It is the duty of the church to let the world see that it does not tolerate open and commonly known sin in its midst. All disciplinary action should be done with tender hearts and with weeping eyes, and the goal should always be the restoration of the offending person.

(5:9) I wrote to you in my epistle not to keep company with sexually immoral people.

It seems that Paul had already written a letter to the Corinthians urging them to avoid keeping close company with sexually immoral persons.

This admonition was especially needful at Corinth since it was known as a wicked and licentious city, and many of the new Christians had lived vile and immoral lives before their conversion.

(5:10) Yet I certainly did not mean with the sexually immoral people of this world, or with the covetous, or extortioners, or idolaters, since then you would need to go out of the world.

Paul was not saying that they must stay aloof from all sexually immoral people in human society. It would be impossible to totally avoid association with wicked people. We would have to go out of the world altogether if we were required to withdraw from all contact with wickedness.

The *covetous* are those possessed with an undue desire to have and to get more. Covetous persons are characterized by a greedy and grasping spirit. *Extortioners* are those who manipulate business deals in such a way as to squeeze the poor. *Idolaters* are those who put other persons or things ahead of God.

(5:11) But now I have written to you not to keep company with anyone named a brother, who is sexually immoral, or covetous, or an idolater, or a reviler, or a drunkard, or an extortioner—not even to eat with such a person.

Paul further explains that it is the purity *of the church* that he had in mind in verse 9. What he meant was that God's people are not to associate with *church members* who are guilty of these sins—and there are some additional sins named.

In addition to the sins named in verses 9-10, Paul includes *revilers*—those who use slanderous and abusive speech. Also included are *drunkards*—those who become intoxicated with alcoholic drinks.

The phrase "not to keep company with"—speaks of spending lots of time in association with such persons. The phrase "not even to eat with such a person"—may refer to the meal in connection with the communion service, or perhaps to the eating of common meals in one's home. There is no way we can tell with certainty which of the two possibilities is meant.[22]

Some of the Brethren taught that excommunication not only barred[23] from the communion table, but that it was to include a social ban as well. The Brethren considered it *a loving act* to correct an erring brother or sister. Carl F.

---

[22] Sanford G. Shetler says that Menno Simons and some of the leaders in the Amish movement interpreted the "not to eat" instruction to mean "not to eat with the offenders at the family table." On the other hand, Mennonites more recently have mostly interpreted the text to mean "not eating with such at the communion table" (*Paul's Letter to the Corinthians: 1 Corinthians*, page 37).

[23] The family of Alexander Mack Jr. did not allow their daughter Hannah to eat with them at the same table because she had been put under complete "avoidance" by the congregation. (See the Spring, 1969 issue of *Brethren Life and Thought*, pages 69 ff.) More details about this incident can be found on pages 238-239 in Donald Durnbaugh, *The Brethren in Colonial America*.

Bowman says, "Failure to discipline wayward members was believed to reflect a lack of concern for their eternal salvation" (page 88, *Brethren Society*).

The prohibitions were not commanded with a desire to hurt or to show power, but to protect the church from the infection of sin.

4. The Dangers of Church Discipline (5:12-13)

The Lord calls upon the church of God to maintain careful discipline over its members within the fellowship. Discipline is always to be done for the glory of the Lord Jesus Christ. The task of carrying out the discipline of erring members has difficulties.

(5:12) For what have I to do with judging those also who are outside? Do you not judge those who are inside?

The difference between believers and unbelievers depends on their relationship with the Lord Jesus. The local congregation must deal differently with each group.

Paul makes it clear that it is not the church's function to act as a judge of those *outside the church.* Those who continue out in "the world," God will judge. He has appointed a day in which He will judge the world in righteousness (Acts 17:31). We are *to witness to* outsiders, but we are *not to judge* them.

(5:13) But those who are outside God judges. Therefore "put away from yourselves the evil person."

The Apostle Paul makes it clear that those *in the church* who practice open, commonly known sin should be excommunicated from the fellowship. It should be done in tenderness and love (not with hatred and cruelty) so that the spirit might be saved in the day of the Lord.

When Elder John Hamme (see footnote number 19, page 62) was excommunicated from the fellowship of the

Brethren in 1800, the action taken was followed with a statement of genuine grief and concern.[24]

Each congregation needs to be a disciplined body. How can a group from any church go out and witness effectively to the redeeming grace of God and seek to win others to Christ—if there are glaring inconsistencies among the members of the local church? Attempts to keep the church pure and clean are proper, but there are some dangers connected with the practice of discipline.

There is the danger of *going to excesses*. In the early history of America, members of some Protestant churches were whipped and put to jail for breaking the church's rules. In all exercise of discipline, love must abound and patience must prevail.

There is also the danger of *no discipline at all*. In many churches, members can openly cheat and lie and commit all kinds of immorality—and nothing is done about it. The secular world is not favorably impressed by a church whose members are no different from the society around them.

There are many in our churches today who think that they can live their lives just as they please and yet expect to be regarded as being in good standing in the congregation. Some churches are diligent about teaching the Word of God, but they continue to allow individual members to order their lives largely as they please. Many times the person in the church who has violated Bible standards is defended by family members and friends under

---

[24] The Minutes of the 1800 Annual Meeting explain that the larger church looked upon the need to discipline Elder Hamme "with sadness and heartfelt grief," and they sincerely wished that God would bestow upon all His great mercy. The entire statement is found in the *Minutes of the Annual Meetings of the Church of the Brethren: 1778-1909*, page 23.

the guise of broadmindedness and brotherly love, and no discipline is administered.

Over the past several decades, standards for receiving members into the church have been lowered time and again, and yet our churches are losing members on a larger scale than ever. There are many thinking people who long to fellowship in a congregation that stands for purity and uprightness among its members.

When a member of the congregation openly commits an immoral act, it disgraces the church, and the church suffers a loss of influence in the community. If those who sin openly—will repent publicly, the church should graciously and quickly forgive. But if erring members (after being tactfully confronted) do not confess their faults, expulsion from the local fellowship is the only biblical alternative.

All discipline must be done with the motives of love[25] and tenderness, but sin must not be glossed over and excused.

---

[25] John MacArthur offers this insight: "Discipline is not *inconsistent* with love. It is *lack of discipline*, in fact, that is inconsistent with love. 'Those whom the Lord loves He disciplines, and He scourges every son whom He receives' (Heb. 12:6) [NASB]. The Lord disciplines his children because he loves them, and we will discipline our brothers and sisters in the Lord if we truly love...them" (page 125, John MacArthur, *I Corinthians*).

Chapter 5

LAWSUITS AND MORAL PURITY
1 Corinthians 6:1-20

Many of us saw what was reported in *Newsweek* (12-15-2003). Multitudes in our society are suing others for slander and libel, for medical malpractice, and to collect money owed them by others. At Corinth, even *grievances between Christians* were being taken to the civil courts for settlement. Paul says that believers are destined to judge the world and to judge angels, therefore, the matter of settling trivial disagreements between fellow Christians should be cared for within the abilities of the local church.

1. The Scandal of Going to Law (6:1-4)

The letter to the Corinthians has sometimes been described as "a straight letter to a crooked church." First Corinthians 6 reveals one more area of failure on the part of members of the church at Corinth. Christians at Corinth were suing each other. They were seeking settlement of their disputes with other believers by going before the law courts of the world. But instead of going before the pagan law courts, Paul instructed them to get the help of some unbiased brothers in the church.

(6:1) Dare any of you, having a matter against another, go to law before the unrighteous, and not before the saints?

The Greeks were famous for their love of going to law to settle differences. Litigation was a part of everyday life in Corinth. Now *the Christians*, who quarreled about temporal matters, were dragging other Christians into the world's law courts to settle differences.

Initiating a lawsuit is contrary to the spirit of Christianity and completely at odds with the doctrine of nonresistance.[26] It is saying to the world, "We Christians are inclined to be just as covetous, just as quarrelsome, just as disposed to bickering, just as demanding of our rights, and just as concerned about having our own way—as the rest of the world is."

The word "unrighteous" does not suggest that the court judges in Corinth were unjust, but obviously implies that they had not experienced salvation through faith in the Lord Jesus Christ.

(6:2) Do you not know that the saints will judge the world? And if the world will be judged by you, are you unworthy to judge the smallest matters?

The saints will in some way reign with Christ in the future. This fact is expressed in passages like Matthew 19:28, 2 Timothy 2:12, and Revelation 2:26.

The saved believers will "judge the world." The same world that has called us "narrow," "bigoted," "out-of-date," and "escapists from reality"—that world with all its sin and ungodliness and immorality—will come under the judgment of God, and we will be participants with the Lord in executing the judgment. Paul says, "If this is to be part of your ultimate destiny, then why are you not settling your own disputes in the church?"

(6:3) Do you not know that we shall judge angels? How much more, things that pertain to this life?

---

[26] J. C. Wenger, writing on "Love, not litigation," says, "In view of all this clear teaching from the Word of God, Christians find it impossible to do harm unto anyone, to retaliate, to engage in strife, or even to sue at the law. They do not refrain from these activities merely to follow the letter of Scripture, but...being born again makes an individual desire to follow the higher law of Christ rather than his own nature which...would seek to lead him to retaliate" (*Separated Unto God*, page 157).

Some angels will come under the judgment of God. Exactly when the judgment will occur is not revealed in the Scriptures. We note references to the fact in passages like Matthew 25:41, Jude 6, and 2 Peter 2:4. If believers will have part in judging angels, then surely they ought to be able to settle petty disputes that arise in the church.

(6:4) If then you have judgments concerning things pertaining to this life, do you appoint those who are least esteemed by the church to judge?

In the original Greek there is no way of determining whether these words are a question (NKJV) or a stated command (KJV). If verse 4 *is a question*, then the "least esteemed" are the secular judges. Worldly judges do not have a high standing in the church.

If verse 4 *is a command*, then the "least esteemed" are some of the less regarded members of the church. Either way, disputes over small matters (verse 2) ought not arise among Christians. But if they do arise, such personal matters do not require trained legal minds and should be settled by the intervention of some mutual believers, as implied in verses 5 and 6.

This admonition to the church does not belittle the secular courts of law. These words are not a show of disrespect for the courts of the land. The law courts serve a useful function in an unregenerate society.

2. The Remedy Instead of Going to Law (6:5-8)

These verses make it very clear that in the plan of God, settling differences between Christians before heathen courts is utterly shameful. Believers should practice the virtues of self-denial and non-resistance, rather than demanding their rights. The Apostle Paul took seriously the teachings of Jesus who admonished His followers to turn the other cheek and to go the second mile. These were marks of non-retaliation and non-resistance.[27]

(6:5-6) I say this to your shame. Is it so, that there is not a wise man among you, not even one, who will be able to judge between his brethren? But brother goes to law against brother, and that before unbelievers!

To have disputes between fellow believers is bad enough, but that their disputes should be brought to court before unbelievers is disgraceful. To go to the world for the solution of controversies among Christians is an admission of the church's failure.

(6:7) Now therefore, it is already an utter failure for you that you go to law against one another. Why do you not rather accept wrong? Why do you not rather let yourselves be cheated?

Paul says, "Why do you not rather suffer injustice and put up with injury, rather than suffer spiritual damage? Even if you don't know another Christian who can be called to help resolve the case—there is another way out! Why do you not rather accept wrong?"[28]

The instruction given in verse 7 is a bitter pill for many of us to swallow. Rather than go to law and assert our rights; rather than stand upon our just claims—why not simply accept wrong?

Be willing to suffer wrong. Take the loss rather than bring reproach upon the cause of Christ. Jesus did that. It is

---

[27] See Matthew 5:38-42 and Romans 12:17-21. Jesus taught "a more excellent way." He spoke of turning the other cheek and of going the second mile. If someone sues you at the law and takes away your tunic (coat), "let him have your cloak also" (Matthew 5:40).

[28] The Brethren already in 1853 answered a query asking, "How is it considered when a brother goes to law in order to collect money due him?" The answer: "Considered, that it is not in accordance with the gospel to make use of the law to collect money, and that it is wrong for brethren to justify it" (*Minutes of the Annual Meeting of the Church of the Brethren: 1778-1909*, page 139).

recorded in Philippians 2:5-11 and 1 Peter 2:23-24. It is expected that, as Christians, we will agree to give up our rights, rather than go to law before the unbelieving world in order to keep them.[29]

(6:8) No, you yourselves do wrong and cheat, and you do these things to your brethren!

For Christians to take petty disagreements before pagan law courts is not Christ-like conduct. Christians need to re-learn what it means "to suffer wrongs."

First Corinthians 6 does not necessarily teach that a Christian should *never* go to law. It is quite impossible at times to avoid it. Even the Apostle Paul, when falsely accused, said, "I appeal to Caesar." Paul stood upon his natural rights as a Roman citizen—but to take our petty grievances before the world's law courts is forbidden.[30]

3. Violations of Christian Moral Standards (6:9-17)

The Lord is concerned about the whole of our daily conduct. We are given in this section a list of immoralities which will shut people out of the kingdom of God. Christians are to conduct their lives following the principles of moral uprightness. The list of vices begins at verse 9.

---

[29] John MacArthur tells of a Christian attorney who has over the years urged Christians to drop lawsuits that were threatened against each other. In more than 90% of the cases he has been successful. He says that without exception all those believers who chose to drop the lawsuits have been blessed afterward. Likewise, without exception, those who chose to resolve the disputes in court have become bitter and resentful. (See *The MacArthur New Testament Commentary: 1 Corinthians*, page 140.)

[30] The most complete Annual Conference statement on litigation was given in 1920. Members of the Church are not to sue each other at the law. When a conflict arises with someone outside the church, the member is to seek the counsel of the gathered church, and act in accord with their advice. See *Minutes of the Annual Conference of the Church of the Brethren,* held at Sedalia, Missouri, June, 1920. See also pages 728-729 in *The Brethren Encyclopedia.*

(6:9-10) Do you not know that the unrighteous will not inherit the kingdom of God? Do not be deceived. Neither fornicators, nor idolaters, nor adulterers, nor homosexuals, nor sodomites, nor thieves, nor covetous, nor drunkards, nor revilers, nor extortioners will inherit the kingdom of God.

The Christians at Corinth were not willing to accept wrongs initiated against them by others, yet at the same time they themselves were committing wrongs against God and their fellow believers. Paul gives a list of those sins which were prevailing at Corinth:

The word *fornicators* here[31] refers to unmarried persons who practice illicit sexual intercourse. *Adulterers* are married persons who indulge in sexual acts outside the marriage bond. *Idolaters* are those who worship false gods and false religious systems. *Homosexuals*[32] are those who corrupt normal male-female sexual roles. The word includes sex change, homosexuality, and other gender perversions. *Sodomites*[33] are those who practice acts of sodomy, and who seek sexual gratification with persons of the same sex. *Thieves* are greedy persons who steal what does not belong to them. The *covetous* person has an undue desire for money and material things—and is seldom satisfied with his income and possessions. *Drunkards* are those addicted to alcoholic beverages. *Revilers* use harsh speech against others and wound with a careless tongue.

---

[31] The word "fornication" (*pornia*) often speaks of sexual immorality in general, referring to all types of immoral conduct—but when the words "fornication" and "adultery" are used in the same contest, then fornication refers to pre-marital immorality.

[32] The Greek word *malakos* literally means "soft to the touch; a male who submits his body to unnatural lewdness" (J. H. Thayer, *Greek-English Lexicon of the New Testament*, page 387).

[33] The Greek word *arsenokoitai* literally means "a man who goes to bed with a male; a male prostitute" (*Analytical Greek Lexicon*, Harper, page 53). There are no statements in the Scriptures that approve homosexual activity.

Extortioners take unfair advantage of others to promote their own financial gain.

Verse 9 says that those who practice these sins *will not inherit the kingdom of God*. Such persons are not saved—because they are not right with God.

(6:11) And such were some of you. But you were washed, but you were sanctified, but you were justified in the name of the Lord Jesus and by the Spirit of our God.

Some of the people in the church at Corinth were at one time caught up in many of the sins named in verses 9 and 10. They *used to live* that way, but now by the grace of God they had said farewell to such vices.

The tremendous revolution brought about by the early preaching of the gospel is implied in the words of verse 11. It takes the mighty power of the Spirit of God to turn people away from their sins and make them members of Christ's church.

In the passage, Paul describes spiritual conversion by naming three special transactions that occur at the time when the Lord saves us.[34]

The word *washed* speaks of new life, and refers to spiritual cleansing symbolized by water baptism. The word *sanctified* speaks of new behavior, and refers to being made holy inwardly (while by the Spirit's power we grow in righteous living outwardly). The word *justified* speaks of a new standing before God—being counted righteous on the basis of the work of the Lord Jesus on the cross for us.

---

[34] Brethren commentator L. W. Teeter says, "All this clearly embraces conversion—a change from sinners to saints. The style of language here used would indicate repetition of thought. However, the order is in harmony with the order of Gospel teaching. Faith and repentance are implied before 'washed,' equal to baptism; 'sanctified,' equal to the gift of the Holy Ghost, implying also separation or remission of sins (comp. Acts 2:38) and adoption into the family of God" (*New Testament Commentary*, Volume 2, page 101).

When He suffered on the cross, Jesus in that act provided for our transformation and eternal salvation.

Beginning with verse 12, we are given some further teaching about the Christian view of sexual morality in general.

(6:12) All things are lawful for me, but all things are not helpful. All things are lawful for me, but I will not be brought under the power of any.

Paul was a champion of Christian liberty, but here we are told that Christian liberty must be safeguarded by two principles. The first is the principle of *expediency*. Does the action we are deciding to take prove beneficial?[35] The second is the principle of *self-mastery*. Will the action we decide to take make a slave out of us? It is perfectly right to eat, to have occupations, and to engage in recreation—but when they become our masters, at that point they become sinful.

The statement "All things are lawful for me" was likely a common slogan among Corinthian church members who used the concept to justify a variety of illegitimate activities—but it was based on a false view of Christian freedom. True believers have a marvelous liberty in Christ, but we do not have liberty to do wrong! Christian liberty is not a license to become immoral and impure.

Many activities in themselves are neutral—neither good nor bad. And even though all things may be lawful, not all are helpful. We must guard against becoming enslaved to (or, "falling under the power of") commercial

---

[35] The owner of a business could, if he wanted to, leave his office at 2 o-clock in the afternoon and spend the rest of the day at the golf course. Such a course would be perfectly "lawful" no doubt, but it would hardly be "expedient." It would not "edify" or build up his business. It might have a poor effect on the morale of his employees.

sports and television and making money and gourmet eating, and a host of other activities that can be dangerous.

(6:13) Foods for the stomach and the stomach for foods, but God will destroy both it and them. Now the body is not for sexual immorality but for the Lord, and the Lord for the body.

"Foods for the stomach and the stomach for foods" was another commonly used slogan in Corinth. Some used these words to convey the idea that sexual pleasure was meant to be enjoyed, just as food was meant to satisfy the cravings of the stomach.

Sensuality is to sex what *gluttony* is to eating. Paul says that both are sinful activities, and both bring harmful consequences. However, gluttony basically harms only the individual who over-eats. Sensuality affects more than one person. Those who engage in illicit sex harm themselves and the other person involved in the act. Thus at least two persons can experience physical and emotional damage.

No sins are more enslaving than sexual sins. The more one engages in sexual sins, the more the immoral conduct will seek to control the individual. Many today, like those at Corinth, consider it valid to treat sex as an appetite to be satisfied, and not as a gift to be cherished and to be used carefully.

(6:14) And God both raised up the Lord and will also raise us up by His power.

Our bodies are designed to serve the Lord not only in this life, but also in the life to come. Our bodies will be resurrected some day—and while the new resurrected body will in some ways be changed and glorified—there will be a continuity between what our bodies are like now and what they will be like in the next world. We must resolve to keep our bodies clean and pure.

(6:15-17) Do you not know that your bodies are members of Christ? Shall I then take the members of Christ and make them members of a harlot? Certainly not! Or do you not know that he who is joined to a harlot is one body with her? For "the two," He says, "shall become one flesh." But he who is joined to the Lord is one spirit with Him.

To be identified with a harlot by means of a sexual union often lets the man feel contempt for her; he actually uses her only as a lump of flesh, and does not usually respect her as a person. Yet relationships with prostitutes are not as casual as they may seem to be.

From the biblical point of view, even sexual relations with a prostitute create a union of "one flesh" between the participants.[36] A sexual union (even when taking place with a harlot) constitutes a permanent bond between two parties. This does not mean, however, that the sex act constitutes marriage. If that were true, there would be no such thing as fornication—because as soon as one engaged in the act, he would be married!

The word "joined"[37] is used here (in verses 16 and 17). To be "joined" not only bonds the man and the woman in some undefined unique way, but it also shows *the closeness* of our union with Christ. We are one with Christ and should react to sin as He would.

The body of the believer is "for the Lord" (verse 13). We are members of Christ's mystical body and thus

---

[36] For this reason, marriages between partners who are unbelievers at the time—*are valid marriages* recognized in Heaven, and must not be broken by divorce. W. Harold Mare (in *The Expositor's Bible Commentary*, page 225) comments, "Christians may not unite their bodies with that of a prostitute, for they should understand that sexual relations involve more than a physical act— [the sexual relations] join the two persons together (v.16: quoting from Gen 2:24; cf. Matt 19:5)."

[37] The word "kollomenos" means "to glue together, cement, or fasten together" (Thayer's Greek Lexicon, page 353).

should not unite our bodies with the body of a prostitute. We tend to forget that sexual relations involve more than a physical act. Sex relations join two persons together—and since we have been joined in union to the Lord, we must not form another union with a prostitute.

4. The Practice of True Christian Liberty (6:18-20)

There are several ways by which persons may regard their bodies. They may idolize their bodies, or regard them with disgust; but often people use them as instruments of evil. In the final three verses of chapter 6, the Apostle Paul gives three reasons why Christians should choose to refrain from illicit sexual relations.

(6:18) Flee sexual immorality. Every sin that a man does is outside the body, but he who commits sexual immorality sins against his own body.

The verb "flee" is in the present imperative mood, indicating habitual action. We are to "make it our habit to flee." That is the only way to deal satisfactorily with temptation to sexual immorality.

Believers are to flee sexual relationships outside the bonds of true and honorable marriage (Hebrews 13:4). Turn from it and run! Don't try to fight it! Get away from it! Read the account of Joseph in Genesis 39:5-12.

The first reason why believers should flee from immoral relations *is because of the gravity of sin.* Sexual sin may not be all that much worse than other sins, but it is unique in that it rises from within the body. Its strong drive is not like other bodily impulses, for when it is fulfilled it leaves an intense emotional effect on the body. Most persons who have done counseling have heard sad stories of the difficulties brought on by pre-marital and extra-marital sexual relations.

The Lord is interested not only in the salvation of our souls, but also in the welfare of our bodies. It is His desire that we present our bodies to Him—as a living sacrifice, holy and acceptable (Romans 12:1).[38]

(6:19) Or do you not know that your body is the temple of the Holy Spirit who is in you, whom you have from God, and you are not your own?

A second reason why believers should flee sexual immorality is *because of the sanctity of the body*. Our bodies are intended to be temples (dwelling places) for the Holy Spirit. If our bodies are sanctuaries of the Holy Spirit, then it is a great evil to abuse the body. God's people are to have a high view of the body because the Holy Spirit resides in our bodies. It is wrong to dirty the palace of the Holy Spirit.

(6:20) For you were bought at a price; therefore glorify God in your body and in your spirit, which are God's.

A third reason why Christians are to flee sexual immorality is *because of the high cost of redemption*. Our bodies have been redeemed by the Lord Jesus Christ at a great cost. The Gnostic teachers of New Testament times taught that only the spirit can be saved; the body simply rots in the grave. Paul explains that redemption through the blood of Jesus embraces our bodies also.

The Christians at Corinth seemed to forget that their bodies were temples of the Holy Spirit, and that therefore

---

[38] Carl F. H. Henry gave this testimony: "In the '30s, as editor of a Long Island weekly newspaper, I received complimentary tickets to the World's Fair. In the interim I had become an evangelical believer; my life was now guided by the Star of Bethlehem. The headline sexlet in those days was Sally Rand, a fan dancer whose gyrations drew block-long crowds. My tickets included a ticket good for a peek at Sally. While waiting in line, my uneasy conscience persuaded me that the apostle Paul would quickly find other priorities. I tore my ticket to shreds, and in doing so gained a mile in the Christian walk" (From the account given in *World Magazine*, February 15, 1997, page 26).

they ought to honor God with their bodies. God expects Christians to be models of moral purity.

Some of the believers at Corinth thought they were so spiritually superior that they could do whatever they wanted with their bodies, and so they engaged in a variety of kinds of sexual immorality. Our day is characterized by people who live by the same kind of Playboy philosophy.

God's intent is that sexual activity should occur only within the context of true and honorable marriage. The *New Jerusalem Bible* renders Hebrews 13:4 with these words: "Marriage must be honored by all, and marriages must be kept undefiled, because the sexually immoral and adulterers will come under God's judgment." Sexual relations outside the bonds of a true marriage constitute raw and wicked sin. Such conduct hurts God because it shows that we are choosing to follow our own desires rather than His will. Illicit sexual activity hurts others because it deeply affects the personality, and often leads to serious diseases.

British social anthropologist, J. D. Unwin, spent seven years studying the births and deaths of eighty civilizations. He says that in the early days of every society, premarital and extramarital sexual relationships were strictly prohibited. But later in the life of each society, its people began to rebel against the prohibitions, demanding freedom to express their passions. The declining morals eventually resulted in the decay and destruction of each of the civilizations.

His conclusion is that when a man is devoted to one woman and one family, he is motivated to build and save and protect and prosper on *their* behalf. But when male and female sexual interests are dispersed and generalized, their energies and efforts go into the gratification of sensual desires—and the society weakens and falls apart.

We must keep in mind, however, that there are many other sins beside sexual sins. There are sins of the spirit—such as anger, bitterness, self-pity, unkindness, and holding an unforgiving attitude, etc. These sins (when unconfessed and unforgiven) can send people to everlasting destruction also. Thankfully, the grace of God can bring change to the sinner's life. It is helpful to read the words of verse 11 again—"and such were some of you." These words should give hope to even the worst of sinners.

Chapter 6

FAITHFUL MARRIAGE
1 Corinthians 7:1-40

After dealing with the problems reported by the people of Chloe's household (1:11), Paul began to answer questions that had been sent to him apparently in a letter from Corinth (7:1).

The questions sent from Corinth related to marriage and divorce, food offered to idols, the distinction between men and women, the abuse of the lovefeast, speaking in tongues, women speaking in the assembly, and the resurrection. In chapter 7 Paul responds to questions related to faithfulness in marriage.

Some in Corinth embraced the philosophy known as Gnosticism. They claimed that the body is evil and only the spirit is good, so it doesn't matter how much one indulges the body. The libertines said that people can sin with the body and not harm their spiritual lives. There were others in Corinth who said that one must suppress every physical desire. Those who held this view claimed that celibacy was the only proper lifestyle for the Christian.

1. Principles for Married Life (7:1-9)

The first question with which Paul deals has to do with marriage and the single state. The *biblical* answers to questions about marriage and family often seem to be offensive to persons in secular society.

(7:1) Now concerning the things of which you wrote to me: It is good for a man not to touch a woman.

The Greek word translated "to touch" a woman is a euphemism for the phrase "to have sexual relations with" a woman.[39] This may seem to say that Paul is teaching against marriage. But in a number of other places Paul speaks in favor of marriage.[40] In fact, Paul says that to forbid people to marry is one of the signs of the end-time apostasy (I Timothy 4:1-3).

(7:2) Nevertheless, because of sexual immorality, let each man have his own wife, and let each woman have her own husband.

God intends marriage to be a union of one man and one woman for life. Because there is so much immorality in the world about us, the temptations to fall into immorality are very strong. Thus it is usually wise to marry—for marriage provides a wholesome release for the sex drive.

Paul agrees that the celibate state is good, and singleness is not to be condemned. On the other hand, marriage is a protection against impurity. Fornication abounded in Corinth, as it does in our communities today, and so people are advised to marry. It is important to remember that this is not the only reason for marriage.[41]

(7:3-5) Let the husband render to his wife the affection due her, and likewise also the wife to her husband. The wife does not have authority over her own body, but the husband does. And likewise the husband does not have authority over his own body, but the wife does. Do not deprive one another except with consent for a time, that you may give yourselves to fasting and prayer; and come

---

[39] The word "*haptesthai*" means literally "to fasten oneself to another." It has come to mean "to have sexual relations with" a woman. The NIV is a poor translation of 7:1, when it says, *"It is good for a man not to marry."*

[40] For example, 1 Timothy 3: 2 and Ephesians 5:22-33.

[41] Paul is not here writing a treatise on marriage, but is answering questions from the believers at Corinth in the context of their setting. Paul sets forth a more balanced view of the higher aspects of marriage in other parts of the New Testament. Paul, in Ephesians 5:22-33, and Peter, in I Peter 3:1-7, give classic statements on the beauty of marriage in its highest biblical meaning.

together again so that Satan does not tempt you because of your lack of self-control.

Some in Corinth were led to believe that sex was sinful and impure, even for those who were legitimately married. Paul declares that sex is a mutual obligation on the part of the married. The text says that by the marriage vow, both husband and wife relinquish exclusive rights to their own bodies. The wife's body does not belong to her alone, but also to her husband; and the husband's body does not belong to him alone, but also to his wife.

The word "authority" (verse 4) is *exousiazo*, which literally means "to have exclusive claim to." The husband and wife do not have exclusive rights to their bodies. The sexual capacity does not exist for ourselves (for example, for masturbation), but is provided for the benefit of our lawful marriage partner.

The husband and wife are not to "deprive" (verse 5) one another of sexual relations. However, sometimes by mutual agreement, they may abstain from normal relations in order to give themselves to times of special religious devotion, such as prayer and fasting.

This passage teaches that sex is a means of expressing affection—a legitimate pleasure (verse 3), and assumes that it will be a regular activity within the marriage relationship (verse 5).[42]

(7:6) But I say this as a concession, not as a commandment.

Some say that verse 6 (and verses 12 and 25) imply that Paul was unsure of himself, and so they use this

---

[42] It is clear from this statement that procreation (begetting children) is not the sole purpose of intercourse. The sexual relationship within an honorable marriage is for procreation (Genesis 1:27-28), for the prevention of immorality (1 Corinthians 7:1-2), and for enjoyment (1 Corinthians 7:3-5).

concept to argue against the doctrine of the divine inspiration of the Bible, but such a conclusion is to totally misunderstand the text. Paul made a *concession* in verse 5a; he was not at all intending to *command* periods of abstinence. The Spirit of God allowed Paul to give the permission for married people to agree to be apart for certain purposes, but the Spirit does not command it.

Paul, on some issues, did not have a direct command from Christ—yet his words carry the full weight of inspiration and apostolic authority. Paul's words are to be taken seriously, for God in His mercy has made him "trustworthy" (1 Corinthians 7:25), and Christians should therefore accept the writings of Paul with the same seriousness as they accept other parts of the Word of God. Paul flatly declared that "the things which I write to you are the commandments of the Lord" (1 Corinthians 14:37).

When Paul says (in 1 Corinthians 7:12), "to the rest I, not the Lord, say"—he is not suggesting that his words are less inspired than the other statements in the chapter; he is merely calling attention to the fact that these are words not directly derived from the teaching of Jesus.

(7:7-9) For I wish that all men were even as I myself. But each one has his own gift from God, one in this manner and another in that. But I say to the unmarried and to the widows: It is good for them if they remain even as I am; but if they cannot exercise self-control, let them marry. For it is better to marry than to burn with passion.

The summary concerning marriage and singleness is that marriage is a gift from God, and singleness is a gift from God. Neither state is wrong or inferior. Neither state is sub-spiritual nor is either super-spiritual. Paul's concern is that those who are married will realize the seriousness of the marriage commitment.

Paul's personal preference and advice favors the unmarried state,[43] but it is better to marry than to risk not being able to keep the sex craving under control. Singleness is not to be frowned upon. On the other hand, it is better to marry than to be aflame with passion.

2. Regulations for the Married Believer (7:10-16)

Paul (in the latter part of verse 10 and in the last sentence of verse 11) states the clear command of the Lord Jesus—marriage is an unbreakable union of one man and one woman for life. The clearest teaching of our Lord on the permanence of marriage appears in Mark 10:11-12 and Luke 16:18. Jesus never said anything specific about the case where a believer is married to an unbeliever.

(7:10-11) Now to the married I command, yet not I but the Lord: A wife is not to depart from her husband. But even if she does depart, let her remain unmarried or be reconciled to her husband. And a husband is not to divorce his wife.

God requires *Christians* to marry only Christians (2 Corinthians 6:14; 1 Corinthians 7:39). However, at Corinth there were those who had married when still unconverted, and later on, one of the married partners became a believer; the other continued in the unsaved state. The question to Paul: "What then?"

Paul's answer echoes the clear words of the Lord Jesus on the issue (verse 10). A believing wife is not to

---

[43] There is evidence that Paul was married at one time. Paul must have been a member of the Jewish Sanhedrin, for he says that he gave his vote against the Christians (Acts 26:10). The Sanhedrin was the supreme governing body of the Jewish nation. It was a regulation that members of the Sanhedrin must be married men because it was held that married men were more merciful. It may be that Paul's wife died; or she may have left him and broken up the home when he became a Christian. At any rate, he never re-married.

leave her husband, and a believing husband is not to leave his wife. The "Lord" (Jesus) commands married people to stay married. If one of the partners does leave the other, there are only two options: remain single or be reconciled to the original marriage partner.

(7:12-14) But to the rest I, not the Lord, say: If any brother has a wife who does not believe, and she is willing to live with him, let him not divorce her. And a woman who has a husband who does not believe, if he is willing to live with her, let her not divorce him. For the unbelieving husband is sanctified by the wife, and the unbelieving wife is sanctified by the husband; otherwise your children would be unclean, but now they are holy.

Christians should seek to stay married even when the relationship is strained. Even if a Christian is married to an unbeliever, the two should stay married. If the believing spouse leaves, he or she will cut off the one great opportunity for winning the other family members to Christ. If the non-Christian partner is willing to remain with the spouse who has converted to the Christian faith—the unsaved spouse and the children will receive some spiritual benefit from the presence of the believing partner.

The reason for the admonition not to separate and get a divorce, is that the very presence of the faithful partner places a holy influence on the entire home—and that influence, along with the daily prayers of the believer in the home, may be the means of salvation of the unsaved mate. Also, if there is a believing parent in the home, the children will be taught and trained in the things of Christ. The atmosphere in that home will be different from the home where both parents are unbelievers.

(7:15-16) But if the unbeliever departs, let him depart; a brother or a sister is not under bondage in such cases. But God has called us to peace. For how do you know,

O wife, whether you will save your husband? Or how do you know, O husband, whether you will save your wife?

The instruction is clear—if a non-Christian spouse leaves the marriage relationship, the Christian spouse is not bound to preserve the marriage. The brother or sister is not bound to remain with the unbelieving spouse if that spouse is determined to leave. We must keep in mind though that the initiative for separation must come from the unbeliever, not from the believer.

Some in our day teach that the words, "a brother or sister is not under bondage in such cases," release the individuals from the marriage vow, and thus they are free to get an official divorce and marry again. The context, however, implies only a release from the requirement *to live with* the other partner.

The separated marriage partners are not free to remarry. The command of the Lord Jesus (1 Corinthians 7:10-11), as well as the entire teaching of the New Testament on the subject, forbids it.[44] Marriage is a one-man-one-woman contract for life. There are no loopholes allowing remarriage when the first marriage partner is still living. The two become one, and the marriage vow can be broken only by the death of one of the spouses (Romans 7:2-3; also compare 1 Corinthians 7:39). Anything else is fornication, adultery, bigamy, sin.

---

[44] The most comprehensive, clear, and helpful book on the issue of the permanence of marriage is the 528-page volume titled *Divorce & Remarriage: Biblical Principles & Pastoral Practice* by Andrew Cornes. From the time of the apostles until the modern period, Christians of all persuasions took the position that divorce and remarriage cannot take place within the church. In recent years there has been a great change. Andrew Cornes takes issue with this trend and seeks to restore a biblical understanding of Christian marriage, and to uphold the approach to divorce and remarriage which is faithful to the teachings of Christ and the apostles. He thoroughly examines marriage and divorce in both the Old and New Testaments.

The early Anabaptists taught the permanence of the marriage relationship. *Divorce* was allowed when adultery occurred, but *remarriage* was always forbidden if the first partner was still living.[45]

The Brethren position slowly began to change. A major report passed by the 1933 Annual Conference stated that divorced persons who remarry while their former spouse is still living, may be received as members of the church, but are not eligible for the offices of deacon or minister. Later Annual Conference decisions (in 1964 and 1977) did not encourage the remarriage of divorced persons with living spouses, but stressed being loving and not judgmental—and thus opened the door for divorce and remarriage regardless of the circumstances.

Nevertheless, the fact remains that *at no place in the New Testament is it explicitly stated that persons with a marriage partner still living are free to remarry again.*

In light of the massive breakdown in marriages today, the church should do all it can to stress the permanence of marriage, and to strengthen those marriages that seem to be faltering. There will be tensions in any marriage, for no two people think exactly alike on every issue. But God "has called us to peace" (7:15b), and all married partners need to make intentional efforts day after day to get along harmoniously.

---

[45] Kenneth Shaffer and Graydon Snyder summarize the early Brethren view: "Alexander Mack (1679-1735), the leader of the first eight Brethren baptized in 1708, wrote about marriage and divorce in his *Rights and Ordinances* (1715)....It is clear from Mack's writings that marriage is for life. Separation is permitted only if an unbelieving spouse initiated it or if the unbelieving spouse 'were to break out in all kinds of outrage and adultery.' [Mack believed that] when separation occurs under such circumstances, the believer is not permitted to remarry. Mack's primary text for his views on marriage and divorce is 1 Corinthians 7" (*Texts in Transit II*, page 8).

3. Further Counsel on Marriage (7:17-40)

The section of chapter 7 (between verses 17 and 24) explains that just as a Christian marriage partner is not released from a spouse because of conversion to Christ (7:12-16), so a slave is not automatically released from his master when he accepts Jesus as Savior. Those who are Jews or Gentiles need not change their identities.

Individuals who become Christians should resolve to live contentedly where God has placed them.

(7:17) But as God has distributed to each one, as the Lord has called each one, so let him walk. And so I ordain in all the churches.

The message of the gospel comes to people in all walks of life. Some are farmers, fruit growers, housewives, cabinet makers, bar tenders, and so forth. The question is: Must we leave our jobs, our social standing, and our stations in life?

(7:18-19) Was anyone called while circumcised? Let him not become uncircumcised. Was anyone called while uncircumcised? Let him not be circumcised. Circumcision is nothing and uncircumcision is nothing, but keeping the commandments of God is what matters.

The conversion of a Jew does not mean that he must lose his Jewish identity, neither must a Gentile upon conversion, adopt the sign of circumcision. The important thing for a Christian is to carefully keep God's commands.

(7:20) Let each one remain in the same calling in which he was called.

The general rule is that people should remain in the same social situation in which they were when they came to Christ for salvation. What really matters is not one's temporal state, but one's spiritual standing with the Lord.

This admonition has practical value for us today. We should serve God faithfully where we are. Sometimes

Christians rationalize their lack of devotion to the Lord's work as being due to their circumstances. They say, "If only I had worked in a different office, or lived in another neighborhood, or had gone to another church, or had more favorable surroundings at home—then I could serve Christ with greater fervor." But such circumstances are not the issue. Changing our setting *usually does little* to solve spiritual problems. We should ask God for special grace to serve Him faithfully where we are.

(7:21-23) Were you called while a slave? Do not be concerned about it; but if you can be made free, rather use it. For he who is called in the Lord while a slave is the Lord's freedman. Likewise he who is called while free is Christ's slave. You were bought at a price; do not become slaves of men.

Paul did not condone slavery, but neither did he seek to bring a violent revolution to eliminate slavery. As people on an individual basis embrace salvation, the teaching of gospel truth becomes a sanctifying influence within society.

The status of the slave carries no dishonor. Slaves who are in Christ are equal in status to those of higher status in the church. Galatians 3:28 says there is no distinction between "slave" and "free."

The slave is really free from the bondage of Satan now that he has accepted Christ. He is now Christ's slave, but he is *not* free to do as he pleases. Even the most humble work in life is to be done in a way that pleases the Lord.

All persons who can improve their social and economic status *by rightful means* are of course free to make that improvement. "If you can be made free, rather use it" (7:21b). Generally, however, we are to be Christians where we are!

(7:24) Brethren, let each one remain with God in that state in which he was called.

The simple truth is that the gospel is designed primarily to change our spiritual lives, not our social status. We are to "remain with God" and live in the atmosphere of the Holy Spirit who dwells in our bodies. But while the general rule is "Serve the Lord in whatever station you find yourself at the time of conversion"—there are some disreputable jobs that people are to forsake upon conversion. The early church had a long list of professions which Christians were to avoid.

One could not be a faithful Christian in the church of early centuries, and continue to be a bar tender, a race chariot driver, or a soldier in the Roman army.[46] In other words, the general rule is not to be taken in an absolute sense. It is impossible to "remain with God" (7:24) while pursuing certain debasing activities in life.

In the final verses of chapter 7 Paul answers what must have been specific questions about the unmarried. He deals with unmarried people (7:25-35), the parents of unmarried girls (7:36-38), and widows (7:39-40).

(7:25) Now concerning virgins: I have no commandment from the Lord; yet I give judgment as one whom the Lord in His mercy has made trustworthy.

Once again, as noted earlier, Paul is dealing with a situation not covered by our Lord's direct teaching. Paul is not saying that this is merely a personal conviction without divine sanction. Instead of disclaiming inspiration for what he writes, Paul actually claims for his own words *the same authority* as for the words of Christ himself. He says that

---

[46] For a more complete list of trades and professions and activities which had to be abandoned by converts to Christianity in the early centuries of church history, see William Barclay, *Turning to God*, page 97

the Lord in mercy has made him a "trustworthy" witness of the truth, and so his words are to be taken seriously.

(7:26-28) I suppose therefore that this is good because of the present distress—that it is good for a man to remain as he is: Are you bound to a wife? Do not seek to be loosed. Are you loosed from a wife? Do not seek a wife. But even if you do marry, you have not sinned; and if a virgin marries, she has not sinned. Nevertheless such will have trouble in the flesh, but I would spare you.

In the New Testament church, Christians were despised and suspected on every hand. There was suffering and persecution. Christians sometimes had to flee at a moment's notice and leave home and loved ones for Christ's sake. Therefore those who were unmarried might better remain unmarried. One preacher aptly says, "When the high seas are raging, it is not the proper time to be changing ships."

Verse 28 says, however, that if one finds a partner, and that person is willing to share with the individual the risk and the danger, it is not a sin to marry.

(7:29-31) But this I say, brethren, the time is short, so that from now on even those who have wives should be as though they had none, those who weep as though they did not weep, those who rejoice as though they did not rejoice, those who buy as though they did not possess, and those who use this world as not misusing it. For the form of this world is passing away.

We are reminded that the time is short, and so we should conduct ourselves in such a way that we can make the best use of the time available.

The clause "those who have wives should be as though they had none" (verse 29)—means "Live for the Lord *in marriage*; try not to let the marriage responsibilities hinder the work for the Lord. Don't try to dissolve the marriage, and spend your time trying to work out some other arrangement."

The references (verse 30) to weeping and rejoicing and buying—mean that since the end of the age is always near, we are to temper our lives on earth by eternal values. We must not become so occupied with the things of time that we neglect the things pertaining to eternity. If we are engrossed with the trinkets of this world, we are making a serious mistake.

The causes of weeping will soon be over, and God will wipe all tears from our eyes. The present world as we know it today will soon come to an end.

(7:32-35) But I want you to be without care. He who is unmarried cares for the things that belong to the Lord— how he may please the Lord. But he who is married cares about the things of the world—how he may please his wife. There is a difference between a wife and a virgin. The unmarried woman cares about the things of the Lord, that she may be holy both in body and in spirit. But she who is married cares about the things of the world—how she may please her husband. And this I say for your own profit, not that I may put a leash on you, but for what is proper, and that you may serve the Lord without distraction.

Under the present circumstances (verse 26), Paul had advised that it was better to remain unmarried, because the unmarried can more readily give themselves to the Lord's work without as many distractions.

On the other hand, if there are those who choose to marry, they are not sinning (verse 28a). However, those who marry (whether men or women) will place much of their attention on meeting the needs and desires of their spouses (verses 33-34). By way of contrast, the unmarried person can devote more energy to the Lord's work, and do it without being sidetracked as often.

This is another case of divine permission; either course of action is right and good. The advice given here is a principle that applies to many areas of Christian living. Advice may be given, but each Christian must make a decision in good conscience.

(7:36-38) But if any man thinks he is behaving improperly toward his virgin, if she is past the flower of youth, and thus it must be, let him do what he wishes; he does not sin; let them marry. Nevertheless he who stands steadfast in his heart, having no necessity, but has power over his own will, and has so determined in his heart that he will keep his virgin, does well. So then he who gives her in marriage does well, but he who does not give her in marriage does better.

Paul speaks in these verses to the parents of unmarried daughters.[47] Should Christian parents in Corinth arrange for the marriage of a daughter who is mature and fully developed and ready for marriage? Should the father[48] "keep his virgin" [daughter], or should "he give" [*gumizo*] her in marriage?

The advice is this: It is better in light of current circumstances for the father not to give his daughter in marriage. However, one who gives his daughter in marriage does well; one who decides not to give the daughter in marriage does better (verse 38).

And while customs have changed in the area of marriage, it is still true that Christian parents should be

---

[47] There are those who say that this passage refers to a young man who is considering marrying his girl friend. Some translations of the Bible (NIV, NRSV, etc.) reflect this interpretation. But the Greek word *gamizo* (verse 38) strictly means "to *give* in marriage." The word *terein* (verse 37) means "to keep." How could it be speaking of a young man who wants to marry the virgin? He could not *keep* her, for he has not yet had her!

[48] It was the custom in early times for the father to choose the husband for his daughter.

prayerfully concerned about whom their children should marry.

(7:39-40) A wife is bound by law as long as her husband lives; but if her husband dies, she is at liberty to be married to whom she wishes, only in the Lord. But she is happier if she remains as she is, according to my judgment—and I think I also have the Spirit of God.

The Bible lifts up a lofty standard: Marriage is to be a life-long arrangement. The wife is "bound"[49] by law as long as her husband lives.

The reference in these verses is to widows. Death breaks the marriage relationship, and the widow is free to remarry if her husband dies. Paul suggests that she will be happier if she chooses to remain unmarried, but if she does marry again, it is to be "only in the Lord."

The principle stated here applies to any marriage. The Christian is to marry only another who is a believer. The believer who marries an unbeliever violates the clear command of the Scriptures found in 2 Corinthians 6:14-18. The old Puritan proverb says, "If you are a child of God and you marry a child of the devil, you will be certain to have trouble with your father-in-law!"

By way of summary—Some have misunderstood the teaching of this chapter, thinking that Paul was advocating celibacy. But the point being made here is that if the Lord should lead a person to refrain from marriage in order to serve the Lord more efficiently—there would be nothing wrong with celibacy. But when we consider the entire counsel of the Word of God, it is obvious that marriage is the rule and celibacy is the exception.

---

[49] The Greek word *dedetai* is a strong term (second person singular perfect indicative passive of *deo*) which means "to bind, to put under obligation, to fasten with chains" (*Thayer's Greek Lexicon*, page 131).

For those who are planning to get married, be sure your husband-or-wife-to-be is a Christian (7:39); be diligent about marrying "only in the Lord." If you are already married, do all you possibly can to preserve the marriage (7:12-16).

Chapter 7

CHRISTIAN LIBERTY
1 Corinthians 8:1—10:33

Chapters 8, 9, and 10 in First Corinthians answer the question which the believers at Corinth had asked about Christian liberties.[50] Some things in life are clearly right; some things are clearly wrong—but when it comes to gray areas, most of us scratch our heads. One of the gray areas in the early church was related to eating meat that had once been sacrificed to idols.

1. Food Sacrificed to Idols (8:1-13)

In Corinth, when a person went to the marketplace to buy food, among the meats for sale were portions that had been offered to a pagan god. Some of the meat had been left for the god; some of it was to be eaten by the priests; and what the priests did not eat was taken to the marketplace. The meat which had once been offered to idols was usually cheaper than other meat. Many Christians came from the poorer class of people, and they might be inclined to buy the cheaper priced meats.

Some had no scruples about eating meat which once had been offered to idols; others had a sensitive conscience

---

[50] There are certain things we know to be right and other things we know to be wrong. It has always been right to tell the truth and to be honest. It has always been wrong to steal and to murder. But in between there are areas that are neither black nor white. These include habits, friendships, amusements, sports, etc. which we are not certain would be pleasing to God. In such cases there are questions we should always ask: 1) Does it violate any particular part of Scripture? 2) Does it take the keenness off my spirituality? 3) Can I ask God's blessing on it? 4) Will it be a stumbling block to others? 5) Would I like to be engaging in that activity when Jesus comes?

on the matter and could not eat such meat.[51] Some of the Corinthian Christians became arrogant in their attitude toward those who would not eat such meat.

(8:1-3) Now concerning things offered to idols: We know that we all have knowledge. Knowledge puffs up, but love edifies. And if anyone thinks that he knows anything, he knows nothing yet as he ought to know. But if anyone loves God, this one is known by Him.

The phrase "Now concerning things offered to idols" indicates that Paul is answering another question which had come from the people at Corinth. The question was related to the matter of eating food that was once

---

[51] Many today think the issue of eating food that had once been offered to idols is not relevant today. As a writer of Bible study materials for many years, I am excerpting portions from a letter I received from a teen-age girl in Malaysia, written on July 17, 1979, and addressed to me at the Bible Helps office in Hanover, PA. She says, "I come from a non-Christian Chinese family who prays to idols. On Cheng Beng Day, for example, the Chinese pray and offer all kinds of food (including fruits) to the idols, so that dead people would not harm nor disturb them. The food they offer is much and is delicious. They offer the best of every kind of food to the idols.

"We Chinese *Christians* have to 'starve' on those days because we want to set a good example before our weaker brothers and sisters (who think it is wrong to eat food that was once offered to idols). The problem arises when I refuse to eat the food offered to the idols. My family was taken aback when I refused to accept the food, and tried to explain the reason for my reluctance. I find it difficult to explain to them about the Christian faith. It is hard to find words to explain things like salvation, rapture, crucifixion, etc.

"I would like to tell you about one incident. It happened on one of the Chinese 'great days.' I was very hungry, to the extent that I couldn't stand it anymore. The temptation was too great, and I gave in to it. However, instead of feeling satisfied and happy at having my stomach filled, I felt so terrible inside. My conscience kept telling me that I had sinned against God, and yet I kept telling myself that it is not wrong to eat the food, for Paul says in 1 Corinthians 8 that we shall not lose anything if we do not eat, nor shall we gain anything if we do eat. I really felt terrible that day. So now sometimes I stay back at school (though the lessons are over) till late evening, and then I go home (after the meals are over). I know this cannot go on forever. I am writing now to ask you to help clear this doubt of mine" (from Kuala Lumpur, Malaysia).

offered to idols, an act which offended the consciences of some who had recently been converted to Christ.

Paul explains that knowledge sometimes causes individuals to appear to others as knowing more than they really do. There is no one who ever knows all there is to know about a subject. The point is this: Even if you *know* that an idol is nothing, be careful that you don't become proud and arrogant about it.

Knowledge tends to inflate the ego. After all, none of us knows as much about the vast field of information as could be known. We ought to walk in humility, and thank God for what little He has revealed to us. The promise (verse 3b) is that if we *love* the Lord, then God recognizes us as His own—we are "known by Him"!

(8:4-6) Therefore concerning the eating of things offered to idols, we know that an idol is nothing in the world, and that there is no other God but one. For even if there are so-called gods, whether in heaven or on earth (as there are many gods and many lords), yet for us there is one God, the Father, of whom are all things, and we for Him; and one Lord Jesus Christ, through whom are all things, and through whom we live.

Christians know that an idol is just a piece of wood or metal, and it really represents nothing. Idols are nothing but manufactured gods. We know that an idol can neither consecrate nor pollute that which was offered in its temple. So the conclusion is that since idols are nothing, the eating of meat which had been offered them is also nothing.

For us there is but one God! He is the Creator of all things and the Father of all who are in Him.

(8:7) However, there is not in everyone that knowledge; for some, with consciousness of the idol, until now eat it as a thing offered to an idol; and their conscience, being weak, is defiled.

Most of us know that an idol is nothing, but some who are not spiritually mature do not have that knowledge. There is sometimes (among people converted from a pagan background), a lingering belief that an idol was really something. And therefore, instinctively, they feel it is wrong to eat meat that came from an animal once offered in sacrifice to a god. *Their conscience would accuse them of not having totally given up idolatry, if they took part in anything that had been connected with pagan gods!*

There are some Christians who have sensitive, easily smitten consciences—and to them, eating meat which had been offered to idols is a compromise with idolatry.

(8:8-9) But food does not commend us to God; for neither if we eat are we the better, nor if we do not eat are we the worse. But beware lest somehow this liberty of yours become a stumbling block to those who are weak.

It is a pure heart that gains for us approval before God. Eating or not eating meat will not affect our relationship with God. However, if our eating of meat once sacrificed to idols troubles another brother or sister—then we should choose not to eat the meat. We should not allow *our liberty* to cause another to stumble.

The principle of honoring a fellow Christian's conscience branches out into many areas of conduct. There are some who think a dairy farmer should not allow the milk to be picked up on a Sunday. Others object to a Christmas tree, taking photographs of family members, doing servile work on Ascension Day, serving coffee at meals, becoming a member of a labor union, and so forth.

Our Pentecostal brethren in Italy will generally not place paintings (pictures) of Jesus in their homes. They used to worship before idols when they were in the Roman

Catholic Church, and they don't want anything that reminds them of idol worship. So we must be careful not to let our liberty become a stumbling block to others in the faith.

(8:10-13) For if anyone sees you who have knowledge eating in an idol's temple, will not the conscience of him who is weak be emboldened to eat those things offered to idols? And because of your knowledge shall the weak brother perish, for whom Christ died? But when you thus sin against the brethren, and wound their weak conscience, you sin against Christ. Therefore, if food makes my brother stumble, I will never again eat meat, lest I make my brother stumble.

Some in Corinth went so far with their liberty that they ate food in heathen temples, along with pagan idolaters (verse 10). New Christians might be emboldened[52] to say, "If it is all right for him to do it, it must be all right for us to eat in heathen temples too." But when the young believers sacrifice their convictions, they are taking steps that may destroy their spiritual lives (verse 11).

But if (as verse 11b says) *Christ* was willing to die for the weaker brother, should *we* not be willing to deny ourselves of some personal liberties for the sake of a brother or sister? It is a sin to cause a weak Christian to stumble. To cause another to stumble is to wound a member of Christ's body.

Verse 13 summarizes the divine principle. Paul says, "If food makes my brother stumble, I will never again eat meat, lest I make my brother stumble." Paul's attitude is a mark of sacrificial love—and God honors that kind of spirit. Paul mentions the same principle again in First Corinthians 10:23-33.

---

[52] The Greek word *oikodomeo* (translated "emboldened") means literally "to build up" or "to edify." When the word occurs in the New Testament, it is used in the good sense except in 1 Corinthians 8:10. The word is used here in the sense of being encouraged to sin.

It is very difficult to know where to draw the line on the issues that fit into the principle set forth. What is safe conduct for one believer may be altogether unsafe for another. It may be *that I am strong enough to resist* some temptation, but it may well be *that some brother or sister who knows me* is not strong enough!

Christians sometimes say, "It doesn't matter what other people think; I see no harm in (a certain action or habit or decision). As long as it is right in the eyes of God, what is the difference?" We must be careful about such statements, for weaker, immature Christians may be turned away from the faith by those who hold such attitudes.

Our lives as Christians are to be lived in such a way that our conduct is both pleasing to God and not unduly offensive to our brother and sister in Christ. Romans 14:21 says, "It is good neither to eat meat nor drink wine nor do anything by which your brother stumbles or is offended or is made weak."

2. Paul's List of Ministry Rights (9:1-14)

Paul begins (in chapter 9) by claiming certain rights which he could exercise if he chose to do so. He uses other areas (besides eating meat offered to idols) to illustrate the principle just explained. Paul could eat meat (verse 4), and marry a wife (verse 5), and take a salary for his work (verses 6-14). Morally there would be nothing wrong with any of those things, but because of those who had scruples about these debatable matters, Paul voluntarily abstained from all three of those actions.

(9:1-2) Am I not an apostle? Am I not free? Have I not seen Jesus Christ our Lord? Are you not my work in the Lord? If I am not an apostle to others, yet doubtless I am to you. For you are the seal of my apostleship in the Lord.

There were some who sat in judgment, questioning the validity of Paul's authority, but Paul supported his apostleship. First, he had seen the resurrected Lord. This is a reference to the Damascus Road experience, as recounted in Acts 9:3, 17, and 27.[53] Second, Paul was successful in his work among the Corinthians. The lives of people were transformed.[54] Thus the newly converted believers at Corinth were a mark of the authenticity of Paul's claim to apostleship.

(9:3-5) My defense to those who examine me is this: Do we have no right to eat and drink? Do we have no right to take along a believing wife, as do also the other apostles, the brothers of the Lord, and Cephas?

Paul defends his right as a Christian worker to the same privileges and joys as others. The Christian minister is not required to live in some segregated class removed from the common joys and associations of life. Paul had a right to food and drink like other persons do, and to receive these blessings at the expense of the church.

Paul had the full right to marry (if he was not married), and to marry again (if he had been a widower).[55] The other apostles had married. James and Jude and Peter were married men. The Scriptures do not require celibacy of those called to minister the Word.

(9:6-7) Or is it only Barnabas and I who have no right to refrain from working? Who ever goes to war at his own expense? Who plants a vineyard and does not eat of its

---

[53] Acts 1:21-22 lists the witnessing of the Lord's resurrection as one of the requirements for genuine apostleship.
[54] One of the evidences of apostleship was the working of signs and wonders (2 Corinthians 12:12).
[55] Paul most likely was once a member of the Jewish Sanhedrin. See footnote number 43 on page 89 of this book for an explanation of the possible earlier marriage of the Apostle Paul.

fruit? Or who tends a flock and does not drink of the milk of the flock?

Paul's willingness to work with his hands was especially significant in light of the fact that the Greeks despised manual labor. No free Greek citizen would work at lowly manual labor. But Paul and Barnabas both worked with their hands—even though they had a right to refrain from such work.

Paul defends his right to receive financial support from the churches in which he had ministered. That is the rule in all of life. The soldier, the farmer, and the shepherd all participate in the rewards of their labor.

(9:8-10) Do I say these things as a mere man? Or does not the law say the same also? For it is written in the law of Moses, "You shall not muzzle an ox while it treads out the grain." Is it oxen God is concerned about? Or does He say it altogether for our sakes? For our sakes, no doubt, this is written, that he who plows should plow in hope, and he who threshes in hope should be partaker of his hope.

Paul quotes Deuteronomy 25:4 and explains that the oxen which tread out the wheat were allowed to eat of the grain.[56] The beasts of burden were compensated for their work. Just so, Paul had the right to receive wages for his ministry, but most often he chose to forego receiving wages.

God's concern (in saying that the oxen should not be muzzled) was not so much for the well-being of the oxen, as it was concern for the person who labors in the harvest field of the Lord. God had more than the oxen in mind when he spoke the words recorded in Deuteronomy 25:4.

---

[56] The reference is to the old-fashioned way of treading out the grain from the stalk. The oxen went round and round on the grain until it was separated from the stems. It was only right that the oxen were permitted to munch some of the grain when they became hungry.

Those who proclaim the gospel may do so with the hope that they will be provided for.

If God cares enough for animals to let them feed from what they are tramping out, does He not also care for preachers, intending that their listeners should support them and see that their material needs are met?

(9:11-14) If we have sown spiritual things for you, is it a great thing if we reap your material things? If others are partakers of this right over you, are we not even more? Nevertheless we have not used this right, but endure all things lest we hinder the gospel of Christ. Do you not know that those who minister the holy things eat of the things of the temple, and those who serve at the altar partake of the offerings of the altar? Even so the Lord has commanded that those who preach the gospel should live from the gospel.

The servant of Christ who gives much time and energy to the study and proclamation of the Word *has a right* to receive material reward from those who benefit from his ministry (verse 11).

Even the priests in Israel were supported for their work (verse 13), and in New Testament times, ministers of the Word were provided for as well (1 Timothy 5:17-18).

But Paul chose not to use those rights in order that the people at Corinth might see that his service was unselfish, and to avoid hindering the gospel by being accused of serving as a Christian worker for what financial gain he could get out of it (verse 12).

Verse 12 is basic to our Brethren "free ministry"[57] (sometimes called a "bi-vocational ministry"). These are terms used to describe those preachers (pastors) who are

---

[57] The "free ministry" churches follow Paul's *example* rather than Paul's *privilege*. For a more complete look at the "plural free ministry system" and how it operates, see *Brethren Life and Thought*, Vol. 12, No. 2, Spring, 1967, pages 41-50.

not paid for their service to the church, or at least not paid enough to live on, and thus are required to earn additional income in some other way, while giving much energy to the pastoral ministry. This style of ministry often saves churches from the trauma of frequent pastoral changes.

Paul concludes these verses by stating a general principle: "The Lord has commanded that those who preach the gospel should live from the gospel" (verse 14). That is, those who preach the gospel are to be supported by those who believe the gospel and benefit from the ministry. The support may come in the form of free gifts or in receiving a regular salary. When Jesus sent out the Twelve, He said, "Provide neither gold nor silver nor copper in your money belts, nor bag for your journey...for a worker is worthy of his food" (Matthew 10:9-10).

3. Paul's Limits to Rights of Ministry (9:15-27)

In spite of all the evidence supporting the right of a preacher to be paid, Paul chose to bypass the right of financial reward so that he could spread the gospel to as many people as possible without being accused of having wrong motives. Paul could not be charged with running a gospel-racket by placing an emphasis on offerings and using schemes to get people to give.

(9:15-18) But I have used none of these things, nor have I written these things that it should be done so to me; for it would be better for me to die than that anyone should make my boasting void. For if I preach the gospel, I have nothing to boast of, for necessity is laid upon me; yes, woe is me if I do not preach the gospel! For if I do this willingly, I have a reward; but if against my will, I have been entrusted with a stewardship. What is my reward then? That when I preach the gospel, I may present the gospel of Christ without charge, that I may not abuse my authority in the gospel.

Preaching the gospel (for Paul) was not optional. Paul was duty-bound to preach—but the Lord did not say that he had to do the work without pay. Yet Paul was so committed to the idea of supporting himself that he would prefer to die lacking the comforts of life, rather than to accept support from the congregation (verse 15).

When Paul says, "Woe is me if I do not preach the gospel"—he is saying that a sacred responsibility has been laid upon him (verse 16). For Paul, preaching the Word was a divine call—an inescapable conviction. Preaching was not a profession, but a passion! The true minister of the Word has a message and he must deliver it! God-called preachers sense that the Bible message is like a fire in their bones, and they must speak (Jeremiah 20:9).

Another reason why Paul declined financial support while working at Corinth was related to the deep satisfaction he found in doing the Lord's work without remuneration (verse 17). Many of those who have served in the non-salaried ministry have discovered a great satisfaction in simply doing what they believe God wants them to do. *This sense of fulfillment* itself is a great reward.

What Paul is doing in this passage is giving an example of self-denial for the good of others. He was choosing to forego his right to financial support as a preacher (verse 18), in keeping with the principle he had been teaching back in chapter 8, verse 13

(9:19-23) For though I am free from all men, I have made myself a servant to all, that I might win the more; and to the Jews I became as a Jew, that I might win Jews; to those who are under the law, as under the law, that I might win those who are under the law; to those who are without law, as without law (not being without law toward God, but under law toward Christ), that I might win those who are without law; to the weak I became as weak, that I might win

the weak. I have become all things to all men, that I might by all means save some. Now this I do for the gospel's sake, that I may be partaker of it with you.

Paul's motive was winning people to faith in Christ; it was not his desire to make money and secure an easy life. Paul was "a servant" seeking to help people (verse 19).[58] He was one who did the work, even though others might get the credit and the attention.

For the sake of winning Jews, Paul conformed (in neutral matters) to the practices of Jewish law (verse 20). But Paul no longer felt bound to keep up the practice of circumcision or the Jewish dietary laws, etc.—yet he did have Timothy circumcised, for example, to help remove the cause of offense to the Jews (Acts 16:3).

In order to win the Gentiles, Paul disregarded any attempt to keep all the Jewish practices. To describe non-Jews as "without law" (verse 21a) does not mean that the Gentiles were necessarily lawless, but they did not make any attempt to live by *Jewish* laws. And when Paul mentions that he became "as without law" (verse 21a), he hastens to add that he is still under *Christ's* law. That is, Paul was still under the law of grace.[59]

In order to win "the weak" (those who were overly scrupulous about many detailed matters), Paul was willing to restrict his own liberty. He chose to try and identify with people where they were. When he said, "I have become all things to all men that I might by all means save some" (verse 22b)—he was not saying, "I am willing to become

---

[58] In addition to the information mentioned in footnote #57 (page 109), see James F. Myer, "The Plural Non-salaried Ministry" in the *BRF Witness* Vol. 10, No. 2, 1975.

[59] Even though we are not governed by the Law of Moses, we are not lawless, but we function under the law of Christ.

worldly in order to save the worldly." He was not saying that we should engage in *sinful actions* to try and save souls. Paul never drank or cursed or smoked in order to testify more effectively to the worldly crowd. He never joined himself to harlots in order to witness to them!

To win people to Christ does often take time, and sometimes it involves inconvenience. We must spend time in association with people—sometimes rearranging our schedules so that we can throw ourselves into the interests of other people. We can testify for Christ perhaps by helping a farmer milk his cows, or by speaking words of sympathy to those who are in the midst of bereavement. We cannot join unsaved people in their sins, but we should use any legitimate means so that we may "by all means save some"—and some day they may become co-partakers[60] in the gospel with us (verses 22b-23).

(9:24-25) Do you not know that those who run in a race all run, but one receives the prize? Run in such a way that you may obtain it. And everyone who competes for the prize is temperate in all things. Now they do it to obtain a perishable crown, but we for an imperishable crown.

In the last verses of chapter 9 Paul makes a strong case for the practice of self-denial and disciplined living. In verse 24, the Christian life is like running a race—a foot-race in a stadium. In the athletic contests only one person in each event received a prize—a crown made of ivy and pine leaves, which soon faded. In the Kingdom of God, every child of God has the possibility for success—and the prize is "an inheritance...that does not fade away, reserved in heaven for you" (1 Peter 1:4).

---

[60] The Greek word translated "partaker" (9:23) is *synkoinonos*—meaning "fellowship." Those who are saved may become flaming evangelists and some day will inhabit Heaven along with the individual who led them to Christ.

The appeal in verse 25 is that all believers should exert themselves to the fullest extent so that we "may obtain" the prize. The word "temperate" refers to rugged discipline. The NIV translates the word "strict training." Athletes preparing for a contest practice rigid discipline—observing regulations of diet, doing exercises every day, and cutting out some of the pleasures of life—all in order to keep in shape and sharpen their skills for the contest. The Christian race requires a similar discipline.

Self-control is not easy because personal discipline runs contrary to human nature. But discipline can be more and more achieved as we choose to walk in the Spirit (Galatians 5:16). To be victorious in the Christian race we must continue to discipline our way of living, and some day we shall hear the Lord's comforting words, "well done" (Matthew 25:21,23).

(9:26-27) Therefore I run thus: not with uncertainty. Thus I fight: not as one who beats the air. But I discipline my body and bring it into subjection, lest, when I have preached to others, I myself should become disqualified.

In verse 26 Paul changes the illustration from running to boxing. The boxer also observes strict rules of training. Paul says that he does not contend in the Christian life like an undisciplined boxer—beating aimlessly into the air. Instead, he aims his blows against his own body, beating it black and blue,[61] in a vigorous attempt to keep it under control.

We live in a time when hard work and rigid discipline are concepts foreign to our way of life. The idea

---

[61] The phrase in verse 27, "I discipline my body" (or, "I keep under my body" KJV), means more literally, "I treat severely my body." The Greek word is *hupopiazo*, which actually means "I give myself a black eye." Also, the word "body" here refers to the whole person—his entire being.

was addressed by a young boy, who, when asked what he wanted to be when he grew up—said, "I'd like to be a returned missionary." He liked the honor and the adulation, but thought it would be nice to skip language school and the rigors of hard work and a restricted lifestyle on the mission field.

Life is too short to aimlessly beat the air. The greatest hindrance to winning the Christian race is laziness and carelessness about maintaining diligence in disciplining our way of life. We must stay in constant battle with ourselves in order to prevent doing anything that will disqualify us for effectiveness in the Lord's work.

The genuine Christian is aware that there is danger of becoming a "castaway" (KJV). It would be very tragic for the teacher who instructs others about the rules to be observed for winning the prize—to find himself ultimately rejected[62] for having violated the way of discipline. In essence, Paul says that those who preach the gospel are expected to live the gospel, and to be models of what the Christian life should be like.

4. The Danger of Self-Confidence (10:1-22)

Using Israel as an illustration, Paul warns the Corinthians that while God's covenant of grace is freely offered to all, *this does not mean* that all will inherit the

---

[62] The Greek word translated "disqualified" ("castaway" KJV) is *adokimos*, which means literally, "not approved." Sanford Shetler comments, "It would be a shame if he, a minister of the Gospel, after having preached for years to save others, would in the end be lost himself. In spite of clever theorizing and mishandling of Scriptures to prove some form or other of 'eternal security'—*falling away* [being rejected, disqualified, or becoming a cast away] is not an impossibility for the Christian; it is a haunting reality. Thankfully it is offset by the grace of God and the promise of victory through Christ" (*Paul's Letter to the Corinthians: I Corinthians*, pages 69-70).

promises. Israel is an illustration of a group that was "disqualified" (1 Corinthians 9:27) and failed the test. The sins of Israel during the time of Moses should be a warning to Christians about the danger of becoming a castaway.

All that we read in the Old Testament about the weaknesses and failures of Israel, and the judgments that followed—are intended for our edification so that we might not stumble and fall in the same manner.

At the heart of these verses lies the over-confidence of some of the Corinthian Christians. Their point of view was this: "We have been baptized, and we are one with Christ; we have partaken of the body and blood of Christ, and therefore we are safe. We can exercise our liberties in Christ and not be harmed. There is no possible danger for us." Under grace the Corinthians seemed to think that there was liberty to live pretty much as they wished. But Paul warns those who speak with self-confidence.

Many benefits were bestowed upon Israel. All were delivered from Egypt and were protected by the pillar of cloud in the Wilderness—but God was not pleased with all the Israelites. As a result of their disobedience, *nearly all the adults who left Egypt died in the Wilderness.* Paul uses this illustration to warn the Corinthians that those who sin freely against God will not inherit eternal life—even though they may claim to be Christians.

(10:1-5) Moreover, brethren, I do not want you to be unaware that all our fathers were under the cloud, all passed through the sea, all were baptized into Moses in the cloud and in the sea, all ate the same spiritual food, and all drank the same spiritual drink. For they drank of that spiritual Rock that followed them, and that Rock was Christ. But with most of them God was not well pleased, for their bodies were scattered in the wilderness.

The clause "all passed through the sea" speaks of God's deliverance of Israel from slavery in Egypt. The words "all our fathers were under the cloud" are a reminder of the Lord's guidance. The words "all ate the same spiritual food, and all drank the same spiritual drink"[63] refer to the manna in the Wilderness and the miraculous supply of water during the years of meandering in the desert. The people knew that the manna was a gift from God and that the water was no common water.

The clause "all were baptized into Moses" refers to the concept of identification. The Israelites were identified with and united with their leader Moses. Their deliverance through the Red Sea was (like water baptism) a symbol of deliverance from the old life. It is not important to press the *mode* of baptism here because the focus is on a spiritual principle rather than on the act of baptism.

The words "For they drank of that spiritual Rock that followed them, and that Rock was Christ"—are a clear testimony to the pre-existence of Christ. It was Jesus Christ (the second Person of the eternal Godhead) who was with the Israelites all the way. The lesson for every Christian is this: Christ dwelled among the people of Israel and did many wonderful miracles in their behalf—yet because of unbelief and sin they perished.

Most of Israel (all but two of the adults[64]) died in the Wilderness. There were 600,000 men who left Egypt, and therefore the entire group was likely more than two million people. This means that nearly 150 adults died each day on the average during the years of wandering. Their

---

[63] The manna was called "spiritual food" because it was provided by a supernatural means (Exodus 16:1-36). Water on the desert was also supplied by supernatural means.
[64] See Numbers 14:16 and Numbers 14:26-38.

bodies lay scattered in the Wilderness (verse 5). The picture of the desert littered with corpses was intended to speak vividly to those who are self-confident.

(10:6-7) Now these things became our examples, to the intent that we should not lust after evil things as they also lusted. And do not become idolaters as were some of them. As it is written, "The people sat down to eat and drink, and rose up to play."

The experiences of the Israelites in the Old Testament are warnings to us.[65] It is one thing to profess to be a Christian; to have been baptized in the name of the Father, the Son, and the Holy Spirit; to have partaken of the Supper of the Lord—and it is another thing to *keep going on with God* and living for Him day after day without going back to the ways of the world.

The "lusting" after evil things (verse 6) is recorded in Numbers 11:4-5 where the people were expressing with intensity their desire for the things they had left behind in Egypt. The "idolatry" (verse 7) is a reference to the golden calf incident (Exodus 32:6). By associating with the heathen in their festivals, the Israelites became idolaters.

Some Christians at Corinth were inclined to do the same kinds of things that the Israelites had done many centuries earlier. The words "to play" mean to dance in ceremonial revelry as the pagans did before their gods.

(10:8) Nor let us commit sexual immorality, as some of them did, and in one day twenty-three thousand fell;

Sexual immorality was an ongoing problem in Corinth just like it repeatedly surfaced among the people of

---

[65] Menno Simons said, "We hope, in any case, that no one who is honest will refuse to acknowledge that the entire Scripture, both the Old and New Testaments, were written to teach, admonish, and correct us" (Cornelius Dyck, *Spiritual Life in Anabaptism*, page 76).

Israel. For example, Numbers 25:1-9 records the fact that Israel began to commit whoredom with the daughters of Moab. Israel also worshipped their gods. Paul says that 23,000 died because of sexual immorality.[66]

The world today is filled with opportunities to commit sexual immorality. God's people must shun many modern novels, pornographic literature, the commercial movie industry, and the immoral material on the internet—for most of it is designed to lead to sexual uncleanness.

(10:9) nor let us tempt Christ, as some of them also tempted, and were destroyed by serpents;

The Israelites complained about their food. It was given miraculously, but was not a varied diet. Numbers 21:4-9 tells about the murmuring of Israel against the Lord for bringing them out of Egypt, and tells of their severe punishment. Numbers 21:6 says that the people were killed by fiery serpents which bit them.

(10:10) nor complain, as some of them also complained, and were destroyed by the destroyer.

These words refer to Israel's grumbling against the Lord at Kadesh-barnea, recorded in Numbers 14:2. Further complaints are mentioned in Numbers 14:36, 16:11, and 16:41. God was displeased with their muttering and complaining. More than 14,000 Israelites were killed by a plague (Numbers 16:49).

(10:11) Now all these things happened to them as examples, and they were written for our admonition, upon whom the ends of the ages have come.

These events are more than just ancient history. These accounts from the Old Testament are written for our

---

[66] The 23,000 was the number killed "in one day." The account in Numbers 25:9 indicates that there must have been additional deaths afterward—and so it says that 24,000 died. Both accounts use round numbers.

admonition. Israel's experiences have been examples and warnings for us. If we are wise, we will learn from the experiences of others. We will be careful not to give in to sexual immorality, nor to express dissatisfaction with our food. We will not complain about our lot in life.

(10:12-13) Therefore let him who thinks he stands take heed lest he fall. No temptation has overtaken you except such as is common to man; but God is faithful, who will not allow you to be tempted beyond what you are able, but with the temptation will also make the way of escape, that you may be able to bear it.

Paul voices a warning in these verses to Christians who think they *cannot* easily fall.

Those believers who do not have many scruples about some of the neutral matters, may think they are strong, *and that* they will *not* quickly fall. But the self-confident believer must be careful. We must not be too sure. The devil is crafty and seeks constantly to trip us up.

David Roper, in a daily devotional, tells about a hike which he and his wife had taken in one of the National Parks. They came to a swollen glacial stream where someone had flattened one side of a log and dropped it across the river to form a crude bridge—but there was no handrail, and the log was slippery. Walking across the wet log was frightening, but they found courage to carefully inch their way across the log to the other side. As they were about to return over the same log, David said to his wife, "Are you afraid?" She replied, "Of course I'm afraid, that's what keeps me safe."

Much of life poses moral danger for us. We should never assume in any situation that we are incapable of falling. "Let him who thinks he stands take heed lest he fall" (verse 12). If we were given the opportunity and the right circumstances, any of us is capable of falling into any sin—and so we need to be on guard continually.

None of us is alone in being tempted and tested. It happens to everyone—but temptations can be resisted. God will not let more be thrown at us than we can bear. There is a way to stand up under the pressure. The Lord will provide the necessary strength to live faithfully.

(10:14-17) Therefore, my beloved, flee from idolatry. I speak as to wise men; judge for yourselves what I say. The cup of blessing which we bless, is it not the communion of the blood of Christ? The bread which we break, is it not the communion of the body of Christ? For we, though many, are one bread and one body; for we all partake of that one bread.

Some at Corinth seemed to feel that they were strong enough to be involved in settings where idolatry was practiced (without being affected by it)—but Paul cautions that they are asking for trouble. Idolatry is a sin like adultery. The only safe course is *to flee* from it; don't play around with it; stay away from it as far as you can.

Some of the Christians at Corinth were taking part in public feasts where idols were worshiped. They reasoned that since there is no reality to an idol, it was permissible to partake of the pagan feasts.

Paul says that to participate in such a meal implies fellowship with the pagan gods that are worshiped. Just as, at the Lord's Table (during the Lovefeast service), we honor the Lord Jesus, and fellowship with Him—so the same principle applies when participating in a meal that is dedicated to idols.

(10:18-20) Observe Israel after the flesh: Are not those who eat of the sacrifices partakers of the altar? What am I saying then? That an idol is anything, or what is offered to idols is anything? Rather, that the things which the

Gentiles sacrifice they sacrifice to demons and not to God, and I do not want you to have fellowship with demons.

Another reason why participating in idolatrous feasts was not permitted—was that such worship was connected with (and instigated by) demons. It is not that the stone or wood image was anything, but it represented a false religious system, which really involved the worship of demons.

The communion of the bread and cup is familiar to all Christians. We understand that the partaking of the communion elements is communing with (and partaking of) Christ. And that is how it was with Israel. When the Israelites sacrificed at the altar and ate part of the sacrifice (Leviticus 7:15), they participated in (and partook of) the sacrificial system in their worship of God. Just so, *when pagan people* eat sacred meals in sacrifice to idols, they are in touch with demons—and the Lord does not want us to be involved with such conduct.

(10:21-22) You cannot drink the cup of the Lord and the cup of demons; you cannot partake of the Lord's table and of the table of demons. Or do we provoke the Lord to jealousy? Are we stronger than He?

The Bible declares that we "cannot serve God and mammon" (Matthew 6:24), yet many are trying to do that very thing.

The pagan meals in honor of idols included sitting around tables just like Christians do at the Lord's Supper in connection with the communion service. The admonition here is that it is highly inconsistent to participate in a meal at the table honoring a pagan god, and then sit down at the Lord's Table in the worship of the true and living God.

We cannot sit at the Lord's Table and enjoy fellowship there, and then attempt also to enjoy fellowship at the devil's table. If we play around with borderline idolatry, we provoke God to jealousy. We must not think that we are so strong that we can outwit God, who has so carefully warned us.

5. Limits to Spiritual Freedom (10:23-33)

The Apostle Paul now concludes and summarizes his long discussion on the matter of meat offered to idols. He states in this section some great and comprehensive principles, which Christians should apply to those questions surrounding issues that are not spelled out in black and white in the Bible.

Paul emphasizes that though we might partake of meat offered to idols without any real harm to ourselves, we must constantly think of those around us.

(10:23-26) All things are lawful for me, but not all things are helpful; all things are lawful for me, but all things do not edify. Let no one seek his own, but each one the other's well-being. Eat whatever is sold in the meat market, asking no questions for conscience' sake; for "The earth is the Lord's, and all its fullness."

In verse 23 the principle of Christian liberty is repeated. "All things are lawful"[67] in essence means that a Christian has the right to do whatever is not in itself sinful—but considerations of expediency and of the welfare of others *must put limits upon his liberty.*

Not all things are wise and helpful. The Greek word for "helpful" is *sumphero*—which can also be translated "profitable." Not everything edifies. There are a number of activities one might practice in good conscience, but those

---

[67] We are not dealing here with issues that are inherently sinful, obscene, or harmful. The instruction here does not apply to those things that are expressly forbidden in God's Word.

actions may not be helpful at all in nurturing spiritual growth. Instead, they gradually lower his ideals and rob him of moral fortitude.[68]

Also, Christians must remember that they have not only themselves to please, but they must be sensitive to the wishes and convictions of fellow believers. Whether or not a course of action is right or wrong—must be considered in light of the consequences that their decisions will have on others.

(10:27-30) If any of those who do not believe invites you to dinner, and you desire to go, eat whatever is set before you, asking no question for conscience' sake. But if anyone says to you, "This was offered to idols," do not eat it for the sake of the one who told you, and for conscience' sake; for "The earth is the Lord's, and all its fullness." "Conscience," I say, not your own, but that of the other. For why is my liberty judged by another man's conscience? But if I partake with thanks, why am I evil spoken of for the food over which I give thanks?

A Christian may accept an invitation to dinner from a home where the people do not know Jesus as Savior, but once in such a home, the believer was not to ask questions about the source of the food on the table—unless someone else introduced the question, or information about the *source* of the food was volunteered.

The principle laid down here is this: The meat itself was not evil because it was created by God (the earth and all its fullness belong to the Lord), but we are to limit our freedoms so that we do not cause others to stumble.

Personal liberties must be kept within certain limits because of the law of love for others. We need to remove

---

[68] This can include actions like spending lots of time attending public spectator sports events, surfing a filtered internet, etc.

all barriers which might cause fellow believers to stumble and fall, or which might keep people from experiencing salvation in the first place.

Two little boys, the one leading his younger sister, were going through a wooded area. They came to a tree that had fallen across the stream and formed a natural bridge. The first little fellow ran across on the tree, and turning, said, "Come on, it's easy!" The other boy gripped his small sister's hand a little tighter and shrank back, saying, "I could, but she might fall!"

(10:31) Therefore, whether you eat or drink, or whatever you do, do all to the glory of God.

We must make a deliberate effort to *eat, drink, choose, walk, and relate* to other people in ways that we know are pleasing to God—not in the style of those who live by the world's standards. We are in the business of honoring God and so we choose to do things in His way.

We are to avoid doing things that are in bad taste and may unduly offend people. Many an unbeliever has rejected the Christian faith because of some careless act, or hurtful word, committed by a professing Christian.

(10:32-33) Give no offense, either to the Jews or to the Greeks or to the church of God, just as I also please all men in all things, not seeking my own profit, but the profit of many, that they may be saved.

We must do our best *not to engage in actions* that harm the consciences of others. Our basic concern is that what we do might profit others, even to the point that they might be saved. On the other hand, a local body of believers that seeks to follow the standards of the New Testament will be in conflict with many of the practices and attitudes of persons in the world about them. This, in fact, is a sign that the church is alive.

In summary—from God's point of view, "rights" are not of major importance. God has called each Christian to live for *His* glory. And God is glorified when we order our lives by His Word, and seek, not our own good, but the good of others (10:31-33).

Chapter 8

HEAD COVERINGS AND THE LORD'S SUPPER
1 Corinthians 11:1-34

In addition to the matters discussed in 1 Corinthians 7—10, two additional issues were of major concern to the church at Corinth and had caused divisions among the believers there. The one was related to head coverings for Christian women; the other centered on the communion of the bread and cup. Before Paul plunged into these two rather difficult problems, he praised the people for their response to his earlier teachings.

Some have appealed to social custom when commenting on this chapter, and they imply that the teaching found here has little relevance for us today.

The matter under discussion in the first part of the chapter relates to the place and the appearance of men and women among God's people. When Christianity spread throughout the Roman Empire, it brought with it a radical change in the way men and women were viewed.

1. The Veiling of Women (11:1-16)

In the Greco-Roman society, women had no opportunity to share the intellectual life of their husbands and fathers, and were often treated as mere legal property. Even among the Jews, the husband had control over his wife. In the synagogue women were segregated from men and had no opportunity to share in the worship services.

Christianity, by way of contrast, emphasizes that women have equal spiritual privileges with men (Galatians 3:28). In God's plan, the woman functions under the leadership of man, but *headship* is not the same as *lordship*.

(11:1-2) Imitate me, just as I also imitate Christ. Now I praise you, brethren, that you remember me in all things and keep the traditions as I delivered them to you.

Paul begins in verse 1 by asking the folks at Corinth to imitate him in attempting to please God in every area of life, and in seeking not to harm the consciences of fellow believers. Also, Paul praises the Corinthians for keeping the traditions delivered to them (verse 2).

The word "traditions" (Greek, *paradosis*) speaks of any instructions, principles, ordinances (KJV), or rules of conduct which Paul in teaching had passed along. The people at Corinth *did* try to live by Paul's teaching; this can be seen by observing that they wrote to Paul and asked him questions about a number of aspects of the Christian life.

Even though women (as noted above) did enjoy *equal spiritual privilege* with men, they also were to be subordinate to the man's leadership in the plan of God, as far as their function was concerned. This order was and still is to be shown by wearing a head covering or veil.

Paul states a number of reasons for the wearing of the veil. The first reason for the head covering centers upon *the pattern of authority (verses 3-6)*.

(11:3) But I want you to know that the head of every man is Christ, the head of woman is man, and the head of Christ is God.

God has established lines of authority to promote the effective functioning of society. The chain of authority is from *God* to *Christ* to *the man* to *the woman*. Man's headship goes back to Genesis 3:16.

God says that in human relationships *the man* is to assume the final responsibility in decision-making. God assigns that duty to *the man*—whether it is the husband in the home, the father in the family, or the elders in the church.[69] Many mistakenly feel that the woman's position of subjection to the man means that she is inferior to him. The analogy in verse 3 shows that this is not the case. Just as Christ is not inferior to the Father, but is in subjection to Him as far as the actual function of His office is concerned—just so the woman (in God's plan) is to be in subjection to the man.

(11:4-6) Every man praying or prophesying, having his head covered, dishonors his head. But every woman who prays or prophesies with her head uncovered dishonors her head, for that is one and the same as if her head were shaved. For if a woman is not covered, let her also be shorn. But if it is shameful for a woman to be shorn or shaved, let her be covered.

Verse 4 says that the man should *show* his subjection to Christ by praying or prophesying with his head *uncovered*. Verse 5 says that the woman should *show* her subjection to the man by praying or prophesying with her head *covered*.[70] This is simply God's order established from the very beginning.

The instruction in verse 6 does not let much room for argument. "Let her be covered" is in the imperative mood. It is a command. It is shameful to see a woman with a shaved head, and it is disgraceful for a woman to have her hair "shorn" (cut off). God is saying through the Apostle Paul that *it is a disgrace for a woman not to cover her head*, and if she rebels against that mandate, she may as

---

[69] John MacArthur offers helpful comments, and says, "The principle of subordination and authority applies to all men and all women, not just to husbands and wives" (*The MacArthur New Testament Commentary: 1 Corinthians*, page 253).

[70] The Greek word translated "covered" in verse 6 is *katakalupto*, which means "to veil." The word "covered" in verse 15 is a translation of *peribolaion*, which means "to cast about." See comments at verse 15 for more explanation.

well make the reproach complete, and cut off her hair and shave her head as well.

The Christian woman is to wear on her head a special covering (a veil) of suitable material, in such a way that it has a clear religious significance.

Another reason for the instruction about the head veiling centers on *God's purpose in creation (verses 7-9)*.

(11:7-9) For a man indeed ought not to cover his head, since he is the image and glory of God; but woman is the glory of man. For man is not from woman, but woman from man. Nor was man created for the woman, but woman for the man.

Paul says that even in creation there is a difference between a man and a woman that puts man in the place of leadership. God made the man at the very beginning. The woman was created *after* the man. This was merely God's order in creation—and that order should be respected and honored in the church.

The sister's head covering is an outward symbol that shows respect for the order that was established way back at the time of creation. If we reject this concept, then we are saying in essence, "God, You didn't do things right at the time of creation."

The fact that the woman "is the glory of man" (verse 7b) implies that the woman is to adorn herself and conduct herself in such a way that will make the man's headship obvious.

A third reason why the woman is to have her head covered is *because of the angels (verse 10)*.

(11:10-12) For this reason the woman ought to have a symbol of authority on her head, because of the angels. Nevertheless, neither is man independent of woman, nor woman independent of man, in the Lord. For as woman

came from man, even so the man also comes through woman; but all things are from God.

The phrase "a symbol of authority"[71] on her head means that a woman properly dressed (with the head covered) may move about freely with dignity and respect. The veil symbolizes the fact that she aims to be submissive to the authority of man and is thereby obedient to the authority of God.

The words "because of the angels" are a reminder that angels (like humans) have the capacity to obey or disobey. Lucifer (the brightest of angels) fell from heaven (Luke 10:18) because of rebellion against the authority of God (Isaiah 14:12-14). The "angels who did not keep their proper domain" (Jude 6) are being reserved for judgment because of their decision to disobey God. Angels observe our conduct (Luke 15:7,10; 1 Timothy 5:21), and if godly women refuse to obey the Lord's command, the good angels might be tempted also to disobey the Lord.

We may never understand the full significance of the statement "because of the angels"—but indeed there are guardian angels who surround every believer, and the veil is a sign that the one who wears it is obedient to God, and thus is an appropriate example for the angels.

Verses 11-12 describe the mutual interdependence between the man and the woman. The woman "came from" the man, in that the first woman (Eve) was created out of Adam's side. The man "comes through" the woman, in that

---

[71] It is important to note that the sister's head covering is an outward sign (a symbol), and it has value only when the heart of the one who wears it is in tune with God. The beauty and meaning of the veiling *must not be canceled out* by immodest dress, or a careless manner of life, or by actions that are not Christ-like in character. For a veiled Christian woman to be domineering, self-willed, unrestrained, loud with words, and shallow in character—is a shameful way that harms the worth and significance of the veiling.

every man has been born of a woman. There could not be a man if some mother had not given birth to him. And so men and women are dependent upon one another.

Where two or more parties are inter-dependent, one must have authority and the other must be submissive. One is to be the head, the leader, and the provider. The other is to be the helper, the supporter, and a companion. The text here points out the reasonableness of God's order, and then implies that we should gladly submit to God's plan for the relationship between men and women.

A fourth argument for the sister's head covering is related to *the picture from nature (verses 13-15)*.

(11:13-15) Judge among yourselves. Is it proper for a woman to pray to God with her head uncovered? Does not even nature itself teach you that if a man has long hair, it is a dishonor to him? But if a woman has long hair, it is a glory to her; for her hair is given to her for a covering.

Every human being has been born with a sense of what is fitting and right—and our common sense tells us that long hair is a glory for the woman.[72] The word "proper" (Greek, *prepon*) speaks of the fitness of things.

Generally, women have longer, more beautiful hair than men. Nature is a good instructor. The longer, more beautiful hair of the woman *is an object lesson in nature* that teaches us that a man is to have short hair and a woman is to have long hair. There is a law written deeply into the

---

[72] My wife and I are the parents of three daughters. We never cut their hair because we wanted to make it easier for them to obey the Word of God when they would later decide to accept Christ as their Savior. Many times folks would remark about their beautiful long hair, and some even admonished them never to cut it. The point is that even though we live in a time when our culture has drifted far from observing God's standards, and wickedness abounds on every hand—yet many people have enough common sense to see that long hair is a woman's glory and short hair is her shame.

human mind, which says that men and women should wear their hair differently from each other.

The clause "her hair is given to her for a covering" must be understood in light of the fact that the word "covering" here is not the same as the word "covered" in verse 6. The *katakalupto* in verse 6 is a special veil which symbolizes the woman's acceptance of man's leadership role. The *peribolaion* of verse 15 is a word meaning "to cast about" and literally says that her hair is given her "for a casting about" (that is, the hair *is not to be* disheveled and hanging loose)—and so the hair is a natural covering, and not the special veiling described in verse 6.

Verse 15 is often seriously misunderstood. Some reason that since *the hair* is given to the woman "for a covering"—that then it is not necessary for her to have any other covering (a veil). But see footnote 70 on page 129. Unless we accept the fact that *two coverings* are mentioned in this chapter, our understanding of it will be muddled.

If "the hair" is the covering that the woman *is to wear*, then "the hair" is the covering that the man (verse 7) *is not to wear*—and that would mean that only bald-headed men could pray or prophesy (preach).

We are also reminded in verse 14 that the man is to have short hair. Men who let their hair grow long are showing disrespect for the commandment of God. Paintings that depict Jesus with long hair are the product of a school of artists devoid of Bible knowledge. The earliest painters did not draw Jesus with long hair. The wall drawings in the Catacombs of Rome portray Jesus with short hair.

(11:16) But if anyone seems to be contentious, we have no such custom, nor do the churches of God.

Paul seems to have sensed that there might be some rebellion against the teaching about the covered and the uncovered head—and so in essence he is saying that *if there are some who are deaf to the weighty and logical arguments just given, then they will have to be silenced by apostolic authority.*

Paul says that the teaching given here was the normal, universal practice in the apostolic churches of New Testament times. The catacombs[73] of Rome and the early historical records all bear witness to the fact that in the early church men were to have short hair, and women *who prayed and prophesied* were to have their long hair veiled. This was the normal, universal practice of the churches in Rome and Antioch and Greece and Africa.

Some say that we must avoid contention (verse 16), and if the practice related to head coverings causes contention, then we should drop it. But surely the Holy Spirit would not use half a chapter of the Bible to teach the veiling for Christian women, and then cancel the whole thing out with one single stroke of the pen in verse 16.

It is a fact that the Greek word translated "custom" (*sunetheian*) refers back (in case, gender, and number) to the words of verse 13, "for a woman to pray to God with her head uncovered." We have no such custom—that is, it is not our custom "for a woman to pray to God with her head uncovered." Thus, the practice which Paul just outlined was observed in the early churches everywhere.

Some teachers imply that the veiling was a mere ancient social practice that was promoted by Paul and carried over into Christianity. But the Oriental custom of covering the face (for women), and the ancient Jewish

---

[73] The catacombs carved in the substrata rock beneath the city of Rome extend almost 550 miles...The many paintings on the walls of the catacombs reveal that the uniform appearance of Christian women was to cover the head with some type of cloth veiling. (See *Let Her Be Veiled*, Tom Shank, page 50).

tradition of covering the head (for men)—were practices different from the teaching in 1 Corinthians 11. The sister's head covering is a distinctive practice designed especially for Christian people. The reasons for wearing it are rooted in the Word of God,[74] not in mere social custom.

There are some particulars about the sister's head covering which are not spelled out in the biblical text. For example, we are not told what kind of veiling should be worn—or when, or where, or of what form it should be. In order that the veiling is a consistent testimony in any given community, the local church should agree on such details.

2. Disorders at the Lovefeast (11:17-34)

In the early church, the communion of the bread and cup was combined with a fellowship meal.[75] That meal, along with the communion of the bread and the cup, was known as the *Agape* (or Love Feast).

At Corinth, the meetings to remember the Lord's sacrifice for us were not for the better but "for the worse." At the early commemorations of the Lord's death, some problems had arisen which needed correction.

A study of the various passages of Scripture which relate the events surrounding the bread and cup, indicate that the commemoration of the Lord's death was a three-

---

[74] The Christian veiling is to be worn because of *God's order in creation*, and because it symbolizes agreement with *God's chain of authority*. It is not the result of some man-made social custom. Therefore John Calvin concluded a sermon on 1 Corinthians 11 with unique insight: "If women are permitted to have their heads uncovered...they will eventually be allowed to expose their breasts...[and] when it is permissible for women to uncover their heads, one will say, 'Well, what harm in uncovering the stomach also?'" (From a sermon entitled *Men, Women, and Order in the Church,* by John Calvin, pp. 12-13).

[75] The noted historian, Dr. Philip Schaff says, "At first the communion was joined with a love feast, and was then celebrated in the evening, in memory of the last supper of Jesus with His disciples" (*Church History*, Vol. II, p.239).

part service—consisting of a time for feet washing, a simple common meal (John 13:1-30), and the bread and cup communion. The three-part event came to be known as *the agape* (the Lovefeast).[76]

Verses 17-22 name *some of the primary offenses*.

(11:17-22) Now in giving these instructions I do not praise you, since you come together not for the better but for the worse. For first of all, when you come together as a church, I hear that there are divisions among you, and in part I believe it. For there must also be factions among you, that those who are approved may be recognized among you. Therefore when you come together in one place, it is not to eat the Lord's Supper. For in eating, each one takes his own supper ahead of others; and one is hungry and another is drunk. What! Do you not have houses to eat and drink in? Or do you despise the church of God and shame those who have nothing? What shall I say to you? Shall I praise you in this? I do not praise you.

It is clearly stated here that when the believers at Corinth came together, it was not the *Lord's* Supper that they observed—but merely their own supper! The words, "Do you not have houses to eat and drink in?" imply that the Lovefeast is not an ordinary meal. If you want to have a picnic, do that at home.

---

[76] Otho Winger describes the Lovefeast: "The Brethren, in using [the term 'Lord's Supper'] refer not to 'bread and the cup,' as most denominations do, but to the full meal which Jesus ate with his disciples in the upper room. A meal had been prepared (Matt. 26:19; Luke 22:13); and while it was called a passover, it differed in many respects from the Jewish passover. The fact that it occurred the evening before the regular passover (John 18:28), and that it differed so much from the regular passover (Compare John 13:4, 5, 12 and Matt. 26:26 to 29 with Ex. 12:14), indicate that it could only be spoken of figuratively as a passover...Jesus had already washed the disciples' feet (John 13:12), and was eating with his disciples (John 13:18-26). It was after supper that the memorial of the bread and the cup was instituted" (*History and Doctrines of the Church of the Brethren*, pages 242-243).

Paul rebukes the Corinthians because there were divisions among them as they gathered together.

At the early lovefeasts, it seems that families brought along their own provisions. The rich brought much, while the poor had scarcely anything—perhaps nothing at all. Those who came with their baskets of expensive foods apparently migrated to one corner of the building (forming a little clique), while the others had their watery soup in some other spot. They divided into groups according to their social standing. This was a desecration of the Lord's Supper, and Paul was seeking to correct it.

The phrase "another is drunk" (verse 21) does not always refer to intoxication. The Greek word translated "drunk" (*methuein*) also means "to eat and drink to one's complete satisfaction"—and this is very likely the meaning here. The lovefeast was not a holiday festival, but a time to prepare for a sober reminder of the death of Christ. The purpose of the Supper meal was not to satisfy hunger, but to enjoy a time of fellowship with other believers before fellowshipping with the Lord in the bread and cup Communion. We cannot be right with God if we are not in fellowship with our fellow human beings.

Verses 23-26 describe the *proper observance of the communion elements.*

(11:23-26) For I received from the Lord that which I also delivered to you: that the Lord Jesus on the same night in which He was betrayed took bread; and when He had given thanks, He broke it and said, "Take, eat; this is My body which is broken for you; do this in remembrance of Me." In the same manner He also took the cup after supper, saying, "This cup is the new covenant in My blood. This do, as often as you drink it, in remembrance of Me." For as often as you eat this bread and drink this cup, you proclaim the Lord's death till He comes.

This section is based on the words of Jesus when He instituted the communion service in the upper room. Compare Matthew 26:26-28; Luke 22:19-20. There are two elements. The "bread" is a reminder that Jesus took on a human body in the incarnation, and that His body was bruised for us. The "cup" speaks of His crucifixion and His substitutionary death in our behalf.

The cup "is the new covenant in My blood"—that is, the cup "is a continued pledge on the part of God that Jesus' blood cleanses us from sin" (page 144, *Studies in Doctrine and Devotion*, Kurtz, Blough, and Ellis). The reference to the *new* covenant is a reminder that the old was a covenant of law; the new is a covenant of grace. The difference between the two is like the difference between the brilliant shining of the moon on a clear night—and the misty moon in the morning after the sun has risen. The new is brighter than the old.

Participation in the communion service is to occur "till He comes." The observance is a temporary ordinance which is to be observed while the Lord is physically absent from us. Some day we will be with the Lord forever, and it will no longer be necessary to remember Him with the bread and the cup. The communion service therefore looks back to His first coming, but also looks forward to His second coming. Those who participate in the ordinance not only look back to the cross, but also forward to the crown. In the meantime, observing the bread and cup communion is an ongoing acknowledgement of the fact that redemption is through the precious blood of Christ alone.

The next section of the chapter reminds us of *the need for reverence* when partaking of the bread and cup.

(11:27-32) Therefore whoever eats this bread or drinks this cup of the Lord in an unworthy manner will be

guilty of the body and blood of the Lord. But let a man examine himself, and so let him eat of that bread and drink of that cup. For he who eats and drinks in an unworthy manner eats and drinks judgment to himself, not discerning the Lord's body. For this reason many are weak and sick among you, and many sleep. For if we would judge ourselves, we would not be judged. But when we are judged, we are chastened by the Lord, that we may not be condemned with the world.

The Holy Communion is a proclamation of the death of Jesus Christ. It is the most solemn act of worship in which the human heart can ever be engaged. When we come to the Lord's Table, our minds should be centered on the things of God. Paul says that to approach the Lord's Table lightly, and to participate thoughtlessly, is to eat and drink *in an unworthy manner*.

During the service, the Word of God is read, hymns are sung, prayers are offered, and emblems are distributed. We can go through the entire service without giving much serious thought to the death of Christ on the cross. To do this—is to eat in an unworthy manner, and will bring severe judgments from heaven.

Some at Corinth were ill, and some had died as a result of their light and irreverent approach to the Lord's Table (verse 30). The word "sleep" is used as a metaphor for death, as it was used of Lazarus in John 11:11 and of Stephen in Acts 7:60. To be "guilty of the body and blood of the Lord" (verse 27) is a frightening statement. It is a serious matter to come lightly and jokingly to the Lord's Table. It grieves the Holy Spirit and dishonors the Lord.

We are to examine ourselves, and to judge sin in our lives, and then come to the Lovefeast service (verse 28). Those who condemn, judge, and correct what is wrong in their lives will avoid the judgment of God (verse 31). We are to judge our inner thoughts, our habitual ways, and our outward behavior in the light of God's Word. And then when confessions and corrections are made, we are to come to the Lord's Table.

The Scripture does not say that it is dangerous to come to the Lord's Table if we are unworthy. We are *all* unworthy—that's why we come. But the Scripture *does say* that we should not come *in an unworthy manner*. We are expected to come to the communion service with a deep sense of our sinfulness and our need for a Savior. Our hearts are to be filled with a godly fear, and we should marvel at the grace of God that brought such a great salvation to a sinful human family!

(11:33-34) Therefore, my brethren, when you come together to eat, wait for one another. But if anyone is hungry, let him eat at home, lest you come together for judgment. And the rest I will set in order when I come.

The Lord's Supper is not primarily a meal to build up the body, but to refresh and build up the soul. We are instructed to take sufficient nourishment in our homes before assembling with God's people, so that the pangs of hunger will not distract our minds as we engage in the solemn act of worship.

We do not come to the Lord's Table perfectly, but we must determine to come honestly.

Chapter 9

USING SPIRITUAL GIFTS
1 Corinthians 12:1-31

The Corinthian church abounded in spiritual gifts, but abuses arose among those who were not very mature. The Apostle Paul felt compelled to instruct the immature believers about spiritual gifts and their proper use.

It is important to distinguish between spiritual *gifts* and spiritual *graces*. Spiritual graces are traits of Christian character. Every believer is responsible for developing all of them.[77] Spiritual gifts are divine enablements that have to do with service in the local church. Every believer has a spiritual gift, but not all believers possess the same gift.[78]

Paul puts spiritual gifts into proper perspective by giving some instruction in this chapter. Chapters 12 to 14 are all tied together by the general theme of spiritual gifts. Chapter 12 describes some of the gifts which God gives for service. Chapter 13 depicts the love with which the gifts are to be exercised. Chapter 14 regulates the ministry of the gifts in the assembly of believers.

1. The Diversity of Spiritual Gifts (12:1-11)

Among pagan peoples in early centuries, it was commonly believed that bizarre behavior indicated a special closeness to the gods. And so it is not surprising that some believers at Corinth looked at those who spoke in tongues as being especially spiritual.

---

[77] For example, Christians are to seek to develop the graces named in Galatians 5:22-23, and those named in 2 Peter 1:5-7.
[78] The variety of gifts will be discussed in 1 Corinthians 12:4-11, Romans 12:3-8, and Ephesians 4:11.

(12:1-3) Now concerning spiritual gifts, brethren, I do not want you to be ignorant: You know that you were Gentiles, carried away to these dumb idols, however you were led. Therefore I make known to you that no one speaking by the Spirit of God calls Jesus accursed, and no one can say that Jesus is Lord except by the Holy Spirit.

The words "now concerning" indicate that Paul is about to introduce another matter about which the people of Corinth had asked in their letter to him (see 7:1).

The words "I do not want you to be ignorant" remind us of the importance of having a true understanding of spiritual gifts. In Corinth, some were not using their gifts at all, while others were misusing them. When the believers at Corinth were still pagans, they served idols that could not speak, and now some of them had carried elements of their heathen background into the Christian church. In their unconverted days they knew nothing of the gospel. They had accepted superstitions, fanaticism, ecstasies, and highly emotional experiences as being valid.

As we shall see in 1 Corinthians 14, some of the immature Christians at Corinth were stressing "speaking in tongues" as being more important than other gifts; they did sensational things to create astonishment in non-Christian minds. Paul was telling the Corinthians that pagans were led by idols; Christians are led by the Holy Spirit, and refuse to worship the gods of the pagans.

The clear dividing line between Christianity and other religious systems lies in the exaltation of Jesus Christ as Lord. Other religions deny His Lordship. Paul flatly states that those who are controlled by the Holy Spirit will never say that Jesus is accursed. On the other hand, only the Holy Spirit can motivate a Christian to say that Jesus is Lord—meaning that He reigns over life.

The real test of genuine Christianity is found not so much in manifesting striking spiritual gifts as it is in living our lives day after day in such a way that they are marked by humility and obedience to the Lord Jesus Christ.

(12:4-7) There are diversities of gifts, but the same Spirit. There are differences of ministries, but the same Lord. And there are diversities of activities, but it is the same God who works all in all. But the manifestation of the Spirit is given to each one for the profit of all:

God gives a variety of spiritual "gifts." A "spiritual gift" is a God-given ability to perform a useful service in the Body of Christ. The Holy Spirit gives *service* gifts for meeting human needs inside and outside the church. The same Spirit gives *sign* gifts for confirming the truth of the gospel in its pioneering break-through into new territories. For example, Hebrews 2:3-4 speaks about those early disciples who proclaimed the gospel throughout Asia and Europe, and explains that God bore witness to *their* testimony "with signs and wonders, with various miracles, and gifts of the Holy Spirit."

The word "ministries" (Greek, *energemata*) refers to "efforts" or "workings." Not every one in the church functions for the Lord in the same manner. We are not all constituted alike, and we do not all have the same ministry (duties) committed to us.

There are varieties of "activities" (verse 6)—that is, some of God's servants are gifted at visiting the sick; others are excellent teachers of the Word; some are skilled at doing those little things that relieve a pastor of many of the routine matters related to ministry. God has imparted a gift (or gifts) to each believer "for the profit" of the entire body (verse 7). Ephesians 4:12 says that God gives the gifts "for the equipping of the saints… [and] for the edifying of the body of Christ." God intends to build the church into the maturity that He purposes for it.

We note the reference to the triune God in verses 4 through 6—the Spirit in verse 4, the Lord Jesus in verse 5, and God the Father in verse 6.

(12:8-11) for to one is given the word of wisdom through the Spirit, to another the word of knowledge through the same Spirit, to another faith by the same Spirit, to another gifts of healings by the same Spirit, to another the working of miracles, to another prophecy, to another discerning of spirits, to another different kinds of tongues, to another the interpretation of tongues. But one and the same Spirit works all these things, distributing to each one individually as He wills.

There is a difference between the *gifts* of the Spirit and the *fruit* of the Spirit. The fruit of the Spirit is inward and pertains to character. The gifts of the Spirit are outward and pertain to service.

Paul lists some of the gifts in verses 8-10. A few more gifts are listed in verses 28-29 of this chapter, and also in Romans 12:6-8 and Ephesians 4:11. In total, there are about eighteen gifts of the Spirit.

The gift of *wisdom*—means good judgment in light of the decisions that need to be made in the Christian life. Wisdom is the art of knowing how to apply the biblical truth that we know. We can use Scriptural truths in such a way that we upset people instead of helping them.

The gift of *knowledge*—is the ability to apprehend and understand Bible truth. It speaks of insight into God's revelation as we have it in the Scriptures. It is always discouraging when people have profound insights into the Word but don't have the ability to express them clearly.

The gift of *faith*—refers not to what we call "saving faith," but it speaks of special faith to act in crisis situations, faith to take a risk, faith to attempt what seems humanly impossible. George Muller of Bristol possessed a mountain-moving kind of faith, a faith similar to the faith evidenced by Elijah when the meal in the barrel and the oil in the jar did not dry up (1 Kings 17:8-16). The *gift* of faith is the special ability to trust God for the supply of specific needs. All of us are to walk by faith; we all have a measure of faith, but not all have the gift of faith.

The gifts of *healings*—refer to the ability to intervene in a supernatural way as an instrument for the curing of illness and the restoration of health. Healing is one of the manifestations of the gift of miracles.

The working of *miracles*—is the Spirit-given power that enables a servant of God to perform an act which is contrary to natural laws—in order to prove the reality of his message.[79] "Miracles" is a word that brings to mind the element of power. The smiting of Elymas with blindness (Acts 13:8-11) and the sudden deaths of Ananias and Sapphira (Acts 5:5-10) are examples of the gift of miracles in operation in the days of the apostles.

The gift of *prophecy*—is the Spirit-given ability to proclaim the Word of God with clarity, and to apply it in such a way that it will edify the church. It speaks not so

---

[79] The sign gifts (miracles) are clustered around certain critical periods in human history. They were most prominent in the days of Moses and Joshua, Elijah and Elisha, the prophet Daniel, and the time of Christ and the apostles. There were long stretches of time during which there is no record in the Bible or in human history of any special miracles. For example, John the Baptist never performed signs and wonders (John 10:41), yet Jesus called him the greatest of those born of women. Certainly the eternal God is able to do supernaturally anything He wills to do, and once in a while even in our day He dips down His fingers of mercy and performs a miraculous healing—or enables a person to speak in other tongues—and thus demonstrates His ongoing supernatural power.

much of foretelling the truth, as it does of telling forth God's message to meet special needs. There is a great need for men who have the heavenly ability to instruct others in the ways of God—from our pulpits, in our Sunday School classes, and at our family altars.

The gift of the *discerning of spirits*—is a special God-given ability to distinguish between the spirit of truth and the spirit of error. There is a great need today for believers who can distinguish between teaching that is genuine and that which is not authentic, because there are many versions of a diluted gospel floating around today.

The gift of *tongues and their interpretation*—speaks of the gift which enables persons to speak in a natural language even though they never previously learned it. The interpretation refers to the divinely given ability to translate the speech of those who speak in tongues into a language known by the listener.

Tongues were natural languages, not ecstatic utterances. There will be more about the gifts of the Spirit as we come to the end of this chapter, and also when we study 1 Corinthians 14.

2. The Importance of All Gifts (12:12-31)

Paul uses the illustration of a human body to explain how Christians relate to one another, and to Christ, in the church. Just as the various members of the human body are coordinated through the head, so the various members of the church are coordinated through Christ who is the head of the church.

(12:12-13) For as the body is one and has many members, but all the members of that one body, being many, are one body, so also is Christ. For by one Spirit we were all baptized into one body—whether Jews or Greeks, whether

slaves or free—and have all been made to drink into one Spirit.

God the Holy Spirit unites every genuine believer into a unit with Jesus and with one another as one single body—the body of Christ.

The *baptism of the Spirit* (verse 13) is the act of God by which "all" who believe the gospel and repent of their sins are united into the one mystical body of Christ. Spirit baptism is a quiet act of God which gives the new believer a place in Christ's body, the church.

The word "all" includes every genuine, sincere Christian. There is no such thing *as an elite group* who have been baptized with the Holy Spirit, *and another group* of Christians who have not been. At no place in the Bible are we commanded to be baptized with the Spirit. The "baptism of the Spirit" is an accomplished fact at the time of the believer's conversion.

(12:14-19) For in fact the body is not one member but many. If the foot should say, "Because I am not a hand, I am not of the body," is it therefore not of the body? And if the ear should say, "Because I am not an eye, I am not of the body," is it therefore not of the body? If the whole body were an eye, where would be the hearing? If the whole were hearing, where would be the smelling? But now God has set the members, each one of them, in the body just as He pleased. And if they were all one member, where would the body be?

From these words, we learn that there is one body but many members. The emphasis is on the individual. We are not to despise our own particular gifts. There is a variety of gifts, and each is needful for the proper functioning of the body.

The gifts of the Spirit are important because each believer has a function to perform in the church. Some of

God's people may be elderly. Some may be ill. Some will be without formal education. They may have gifts which are not spectacular and not sensational, and not very visible—but they have an important part to play in the church, which is the body of Christ.

The human body could not function with only feet or ears or eyes (verses 15-17). Each part of the human body is very necessary, even though it may not be the most visible part of the body—a thought which is developed more fully in verses 20-26.

(12:20-26) But now indeed there are many members, yet one body. And the eye cannot say to the hand, "I have no need of you"; nor again the head to the feet, "I have no need of you." No, much rather, those members of the body which seem to be weaker are necessary. And those members of the body which we think to be less honorable, on these we bestow greater honor; and our unpresentable parts have greater modesty, but our presentable parts have no need. But God composed the body, having given greater honor to that part which lacks it, that there should be no schism in the body, but that the members should have the same care for one another. And if one member suffers, all the members suffer with it; or if one member is honored, all the members rejoice with it.

The important truth emphasized in verses 20-26 is that there are many members but only one body, and we need one another. It is necessary to have diversity in the body so that it can function as one. To know that we do not serve the Lord Jesus *alone* is a comforting fact. We need the contribution of other Christians to minister to us and with us. None of us should say of others in the church, "We have no need of you." In the church, there are many members, but all one body. No one in the congregation should feel inferior or unneeded or unnecessary.

In Corinth, those with more prominent gifts were apparently making light of those who had what seemed like less important gifts. They forgot that *every* gift is needed for the body to function effectively. Even the weaker and less presentable members of our bodies (verses 22-23) are important for a healthy body. Just so, all persons in the body of Christ are needed—even if they feel their role is not very significant.

The "less honorable" parts of the body (verse 23a) may be a reference to hidden parts like the heart, lungs, liver, and kidneys. The "unpresentable" parts of the body (verse 23b) likely refer to the reproductive organs. The Greek word translated "unpresentable" ("uncomely" in KJV) is *aschemona* and means "indecent; related to nakedness"—and so we treat those parts with modesty and properly see that they are concealed.

Because all the members of the body are interrelated, "if one member suffers, all the members suffer with it" (verse 26). If we have a sore toe, our whole body seems to be drawn to that one suffering member, and we hurt all over. There is discord in the body when one member fails to function. On the other hand, "if one member is honored, all the members rejoice with it." There is no jealousy among the members of the human body—and that is the way it should be in the church.

(12:27-28) Now you are the body of Christ, and members individually. And God has appointed these in the church: first apostles, second prophets, third teachers, after that miracles, then gifts of healings, helps, administrations, varieties of tongues.

Paul now presses home the lesson that is to be found in the illustration about the human body. God has appointed some Christians to be apostles, some to be prophets, some to be teachers, and so forth. Eight kinds of members with special functions are listed. There are some similarities to the listing in verses 8-10 earlier in chapter 12. The fact that Paul names the functions in a first, second, and third order, seems to mean that some are more significant than others.

The word *apostles* refers to those who have been sent on a spiritual mission, often to a people outside their own immediate group. In a limited technical sense, the term refers to the "twelve" (John 20:24; 1 Corinthians 15:5). In a more general sense it refers to "those sent" with a message (similar to our term "missionary").

The term *prophets* speaks of those who proclaim the Word of God with clarity, and seek to apply it in such a way that it edifies the church. A "prophet" is not one who merely fore-tells the truth, but one who forth-tells the truth.

The word *teachers* refers to those who have the Spirit-given ability to explain clearly and apply effectively the message of the Word of God.

After listing three *offices* in the church, Paul then names *five other gifts* (three of which had been mentioned earlier in the chapter—healings, miracles, and tongues). See the comments on 1 Corinthians 12:9-10.

The gift of *helps* (verse 28b) is the ability to help those in need. Many times it is the Spirit-given ability to serve the church in such a way that it releases other workers to more effectively engage in their duties. It may include arranging chairs, handing out lesson sheets, taking a speaker to the airport, etc. The Greek word (*antilepseis*) carries with it the idea of "lending a hand."

The gift of *administrations* (KJV "governments") (verse 28b) is the ability to moderate a meeting so that things are organized and people are not confused. The

Greek word means "to preside over"—the ability to steer the church through perplexing issues in such a way that business is done decently and in order.

(12:29-31) Are all apostles? Are all prophets? Are all teachers? Are all workers of miracles? Do all have gifts of healings? Do all speak with tongues? Do all interpret? But earnestly desire the best gifts. And yet I show you a more excellent way.

In this passage Paul asks some questions for which negative answers are expected. Are all apostles (prophets, teachers, workers of miracles, etc.)? The answer is, "No, of course not." All the gifts are necessary. All of them are important, but some of them are greater than others and should be sought.

To earnestly desire "the best gifts" (verse 31) is related to the fact that Paul had just listed the gifts in *descending* order (from "apostleship" at the top of the list, to "tongues" [and their interpretation] at the bottom). It is important that we do not take the gift at the bottom of the list (tongues) and magnify it out of proportion—as apparently the Corinthians had been doing.

We are to "earnestly desire" (put our energies into) the greater gifts—serving as missionaries[80] and preachers and teachers of the Word. But possessing specific gifts is not as important as the way in which the gifts are exercised.

How do Christians discover what their gifts really are? There are some guidelines to use.

a) *Get busy doing Christian service.* Attempt to show mercy, to evangelize, to teach a class, etc. Do what you can, even if it is only a menial task.

---

[80] The word "apostle" more literally means "one who is sent with a message"—and thus in a general way has come to mean almost the same thing as our word "missionary."

b) *Notice if you are drawn toward a certain gift.* Do you find yourself watching the style of a teacher—how he introduces a lesson; ways he tries to make the message clear; and how he concludes the session? That might be a clue indicating an inclination toward the gift of teaching.

c) *Check to see if you delight in exercising the gift.* We should enjoy ministering our gifts. There should be an inner peace about what we are doing. We should not feel frustration with the tasks we have undertaken to do.

d) *Observe whether others notice the gift in you.* Our abilities can often best be evaluated by another person. A frank discussion with another Christian may help us identify our spiritual gifts.

We conclude this chapter with a reminder that we are not to let the present emphasis on *gifts* overshadow the importance of *fruit* in the Christian life. In the Lord's eyes it is better to be godly than to be gifted! Actually, the Lord looks for both. He expects us to exercise our gifts *and to be* godly in Christian character.

Chapter 10

THE WAY OF LOVE
1 Corinthians 13:1-13

First Corinthians 13 lies in the midst of three chapters which deal with spiritual gifts. The admonition to manifest true love is needed to regulate the use of the gifts. However, 1 Corinthians 13 can be a useful study apart from the context in which it is located.

There are three basic words for "love" in the Greek language. *Eros* is sensual, romantic love—the love between sweethearts. It is often used in Greek literature, but is never used in the New Testament. *Phileo* is a natural affection for others—generally associated with love for one's friends and family. It speaks of a strong bond of friendship. Sometimes it speaks of "liking" to do things that are pleasant—for example, the Pharisees loved to stand on the corners of the streets to pray (Matthew 6:5).

Agape is the word for "love" that is used nearly always in the New Testament, including this chapter in First Corinthians. The word "agape" is never found in secular Greek literature.

Agape love is the result of a commitment of the will—a deliberate choice to treat another person with concern, care, and thoughtfulness. Agape love is a higher and holier love—a love that is "poured out in our hearts by the Holy Spirit" (Romans 5:5). It is God alone who can awaken agape love in our hearts.

In 1 John 4:7 we read "everyone who loves is born of God and knows God." That sentence is not saying that every young man who loves his sweetheart, or every mother who loves her children, or every patriot who loves his country—is born of God. Such relationships would be described with the words *eros* and *phileo*. But John uses the word "agape" and says that those who love with agape love "are born of God."

Paul, in 1 Corinthians 13, describes the nature of this higher kind of love. He speaks of the supremacy of love, the character of love, and the durability of love.

1. The Supremacy of Love (13:1-3)

In the first three verses of the chapter, love is contrasted with a number of other qualities—and love is seen to be greater than all of them.

(13:1) Though I speak with the tongues of men and of angels, but have not love, I have become sounding brass or a clanging cymbal.

Love is contrasted with eloquence. The ability to speak eloquently is the skill of playing on the hearts of people by the use of words.

I once heard a great educator, Dr. Philip Lovejoy, give a speech to public school teachers. It was a masterful presentation—but even though a speaker has the ability to deliver good speeches, the words mean nothing unless they are matched by a loving heart and life. Agape love is greater than eloquent speeches.

(13:2) And though I have the gift of prophecy, and understand all mysteries and all knowledge, and though I have all faith, so that I could remove mountains, but have not love, I am nothing.

To prophesy is to forth-tell the truth of God's Word. The reference here is to proclamation—preaching the Word. But without love, preaching is a vain exercise.

All of us have heard preachers who spoke in such a way that they almost gave the impression that they would rejoice in the *damnation* of people as much as they would in their *salvation*.

The reference to "mysteries" likely refers to some of the biblical terms—the "mystery of iniquity," the "mystery of godliness," and the "mystery of the kingdom of God." But even if we claim to understand all these mysteries, and have the ability to discern deep spiritual concepts—without agape love we have failed. We come across as *smart alecks* who boast about our own understanding of God's secrets.

The reference to "knowledge" is appropriate in our age. We have more schools than ever before. The internet in our day is the source of an incredible abundance of knowledge. And yet, the three words most of us need to say frequently, are, "I don't know." But suppose we do know. Suppose we could speak five or six different languages. Suppose we could remember much of the information that the schools drill into our heads—still that would not be as great as possessing agape love.

The reference to "faith" (by which one can move mountains) is interesting when contrasted with love. Our faith can become a cutting and hurting thing. One man who had gone to the doctor and learned that his heart was failing and that he needed some immediate rest—told his boss at work about the dilemma he was facing, and explained that he would not be able to work for a while on a regular basis. The boss responded by saying, "Oh, I have physical troubles too, but the Lord gives me inner strength, and that enables me to continue on." That man's faith became a hurting thing by implying that the other man was lacking trust in the Lord.

(13:3) And though I bestow all my goods to feed the poor, and though I give my body to be burned, but have not love, it profits me nothing.

In this statement, love is contrasted with charity. Charity is benevolence and good will toward the poor and the suffering. Charity is a noble activity—but if giving is done to satisfy pride and to be seen of men—or if it is done out of a mere cold sense of duty, it is not the greatest thing in the world.

In the latter part of verse 3, love is contrasted with sacrificial devotion. Many of our ancestors sacrificed greatly and were so devoted to their faith, that they were devoured by lions, tied to the stake and burned, and covered with pitch and set on fire—martyrs for their faith.

These have been great sacrifices, but the kind of love that Paul is talking about is greater still! Such is the supremacy of love. Love is supreme, surpassing eloquence, the ability to prophesy, and even evidences of great faith.

2. The Character of Love (13:4-7)

If agape love is so wonderful, and if it is so much greater than all these other activities—then what is it like?

Paul explains that agape love is a compound thing. It is composed of many parts, and in verses 4-7, the properties of love are analyzed.

(13:4) Love suffers long and is kind; love does not envy; love does not parade itself, is not puffed up;

Love *"suffers long."* The phrase speaks of patience. It just waits and waits and waits. Patience is the ability to exercise self-control (anger control) toward persons who annoy us. This includes pokey drivers on the highway, people who let their dogs bark all night, and the person who goes into an eight-item express lane at the supermarket and unloads fifteen items on the checkout counter. And then he chats with the clerk, and writes out a check—and we wait! Agape love is patient—it "suffers long."

Love suffers long even when others mistreat us and misunderstand our actions.

It is doubtful that anyone ever treated Abe Lincoln with more contempt than a man named Ed Stanton. Stanton ridiculed Mr. Lincoln publicly, and nicknamed him "the original gorilla" because of his hollow cheeks and his homely facial features.

Stanton said that scientists don't need to wander around in Africa hunting gorillas, when they can find one so easily in Springfield, Illinois. Lincoln said nothing. He was long suffering. And later, when Lincoln was elected President of the United States, he appointed Ed Stanton to be the Secretary of War because he knew that Stanton was the best man for the job.

The years wore on, and the night came when Lincoln was assassinated, and in the room where the President's body was taken, stood Ed Stanton. As Stanton looked down on the face of Abe Lincoln, he said through his tears, "There lies one of the greatest rulers of men this world has ever seen." Love had conquered in the end.

Verse 4 continues by saying that *"Love...is kind."* That is, agape love is generous and considerate and thoughtful of others. One saying that is worth passing along is this: "I expect to pass through life but once. If therefore, there be any kindness I can show, or any good thing I can do for a fellow human being, let me do it now, for I shall not pass this way again." Jesus spent a great deal of time simply doing kind things—even for those who were His enemies. He is a model for us to follow.

A third property of love is that *"love does not envy."* Envy is a feeling of ill-will because of the advantages another person may have. It is a feeling of pain at another's success. Agape love is not envious of those whose health and wealth and intelligence are greater than our own. No matter what we attempt to do in life (whether in the office or shop or classroom or the church)—there will be others doing the same kind of work, and some of them will do a better job than we will. One who possesses agape love does not envy them, but is grateful for their abilities.

Agape love (verse 4) *"does not parade itself, is not puffed up."* Love is not boastful; it does not brag about its accomplishments; it does not seek to be in the spotlight. The Phillips translation says, "Love does not cherish inflated ideas of its own importance."

William Carey was one of the greatest missionaries of all time. He was an expert in language study; he translated portions of the Bible into 34 dialects of India. Yet he had grown up in a poor family, and in earlier years, worked as a cobbler (repairing shoes). One time a noted person in India intended to embarrass him before a crowd of people by saying, "Mr. Carey, I understand that you once worked as a shoemaker." Carey replied, "Oh no, my friend, I was not a shoemaker, only a shoe cobbler."

Agape love is patient, kind, does not envy, and is not boastful of accomplishments.

(13:5) does not behave rudely, does not seek its own, is not provoked, thinks no evil;

One who possesses real Christian love guards against indecency and shameful actions. Those who possess agape love are careful about their conduct in a traffic jam, at the church council meeting, when shopping in a store, and when interacting with persons of the opposite sex.

God told David after his sin with Bathsheba that his conduct was unseemly, inappropriate, and sinful. Nathan said to David, "By this deed you have given great occasion to the enemies of the Lord to blaspheme" (2 Samuel 12:14).

Love does not *"behave itself unseemly"* (KJV)—in rude, harsh, indecent, and brazen ways.

Godly love *"does not seek its own."* That is, love does not insist on having its own way. Love is not stubborn, insisting that others must adjust to its way of doing things. Some people want to dominate most every situation; if they can't have their way, they won't play the game. When Abraham and Lot returned to Palestine from Egypt, there was a shortage of grazing land for the cattle—and that led to strife between their herdsmen. But Abraham said to Lot, "You pick the land that you want, and then I'll take what is left." Love does not demand its own way.

True love *"is not provoked."* That is, love is not irritable or resentful. Love keeps its cool. It doesn't quickly get angry. It is not easily offended. It does not flare up at the slightest provocation.

It is easy to get provoked at the smallest things—when the car won't start, or the fire won't burn, or the calf won't drink, or the meals are not ready on time. If your car or your calf or your spouse had the opportunity to testify publicly—would you welcome the testimony?

True love *"thinks no evil."* That is, love does not keep a record when it has been wronged. It holds no grudges, has no memory for injuries, and harbors no resentment. It is easy for humans to brood over insults and nurse their wrath just enough to keep it warm—but love is just the opposite.

(13:6) does not rejoice in iniquity, but rejoices in the truth;

Love does not find pleasure when another person fails. Love does not feel satisfied and pleased when it hears of the blunders of another person. It does not rejoice when someone makes a mistake—when it hears of broken marriages, or of embezzled funds, or of factions within the local church. Love is not glad when others go wrong.

True love *"rejoices in the truth."* God's people are not glad in the presence of evil, but happy in the presence of truth and of noble virtues. That is one reason why most television programs are simply off limits! We rejoice in the virtues of others, not in their vices.

The person characterized by love is joyful when the truth prevails. He longs to hear the Scriptures expounded, and delights to see lives that are transformed and lived according to the teachings of God's Word. Love rejoices not in iniquity, but is thrilled when the truth prevails!

(13:7) bears all things, believes all things, hopes all things, endures all things.

Love *"bears all things"*—even insults and trials and hardships, without murmuring and complaining. Love bears insults and injuries without seeking to retaliate and to get even with the perpetrator.

Love *"believes all things."* One who loves believes absolutely the promises of God, and is eager to practice all the commandments of God. In relation to other human beings, one who loves is careful to avoid suspicion, and is inclined to believe the best about other people. We are not expected to be blind to the sins of others—but love does not quickly accept every rumor that comes along!

Love *"hopes all things."* Love is not quick to give up; it does not despair. The word "hope" is more than wishful thinking. It is more than the little train which said, "I think I can; I think I can." Hope (in the New Testament sense) is the joyful expectation that someday we shall rise from the dead. Therefore, as the last phrase of verse 7 says, we can *"endure all things."* That is, we will "hang in there" until the very end!

These have been the essential ingredients of agape love. It has been pointed out that we can take verses 4-7 and insert the word "Jesus" in place of the word "love"—and it fits perfectly. Jesus suffers long and is kind. Jesus does not envy. Jesus is not puffed up. Jesus does not behave rudely. Jesus thinks no evil. When we read chapter 13 (in First Corinthians) this way, it is obvious that *love* describes the character of Christ—and becoming Christ-like means becoming a more loving person.

3. The Durability of Love (13:8-13)

Love is unfailing and unending. It stands when everything else falls. Other qualities are only for time; love is for eternity.

(13:8) Love never fails. But whether there are prophecies, they will fail; whether there are tongues, they will cease; whether there is knowledge, it will vanish away.

Prophecies will fail; they shall be done away; they will be fulfilled when Jesus comes. *Tongues* will cease—in the eternal world (where our knowledge will be full and complete), there will be no need for languages of various kinds. *Knowledge* will vanish away—that is, limited information *as we now posses it* will be of no value when we stand in the full light of God's presence.

(13:9-12) For we know in part and we prophesy in part. But when that which is perfect has come, then that which is in part will be done away. When I was a child, I spoke as a child, I understood as a child, I thought as a child; but when I became a man, I put away childish things. For now we see in a mirror, dimly, but then face to face. Now I know in part, but then I shall know just as I also am known.

The phrase in verse 10, "when that which is perfect has come"—is a reference to Christ's second coming. In this life we are given glimpses into the future, but they are only glimpses. We have only partial knowledge here in this life (verses 9,12).

Verse 11 tells us that our present knowledge (compared with what we will know in Heaven) is like the contrast between the knowledge of an infant[81] compared with that of a mature person. There are childish ways of speaking, thinking, and understanding. Parents need to remember this truth when disciplining children.

Verse 12 refers to a mirror. Because mirrors in New Testament times were made from a thin sheet of metal polished on one side, the reflection in the mirror was usually obscure and unclear. Glass mirrors were made already, but they were not widely used—thus the mirror became an example of limited and partial knowledge.

The words "then face to face" indicated that in the world to come, those who stand before God in peace will receive full and perfect knowledge of all things.

(13:13) And now abide faith, hope, love, these three; but the greatest of these is love.

Faith says that Jesus Christ came to save us; *hope* says that He is coming again to take us; *love* says that He abides in our hearts today. An unknown author says:

"Faith will vanish into sight!
Hope will be emptied in delight!
Love will shine ever more bright!"

In contrast to the temporary gifts which seemed to be stressed among the people in the church at Corinth, the three basic Christian graces—faith, hope, and love—will abide forever. They are eternal. The greatest of the three graces is love.

One unknown poet has written:

---

[81] The Greek word translated "child" is *nepios*, and denotes a baby, an infant. However, the word does not specify any particular age.

"Love is *silence* when words would hurt;
Love is *patience* when your neighbor is curt.
Love is *defense* when a scandal flows;
Love is *thoughtfulness* for another's woes.
Love is *promptness* when stern duty calls;
Love is *courage* when misfortune falls."

The whole point of *chapter 12* is that gifts are given as God planned, and believers should be content with the gift (or gifts) that they have been given. The point in *chapter 13* is that our gifts are to be exercised with an outgoing, self-giving kindness that is patterned after the love of God Himself. The point in *chapter 14* will be to explain that the gift of prophecy is superior to the gift of tongues.

Chapter 11

TONGUES AND PROPHECY
1 Corinthians 14:1-40

Corinth was a common center of commerce and was populated by Romans, Greeks, Orientals, Jews, gamblers, sailors, travelers, traders, prostitutes, philosophers, and so forth. Many in the church at Corinth came from pagan backgrounds and were accustomed to the practice of ecstatic utterances. In their unconverted days, the worship of the gods and goddesses involved drinking and dancing themselves into frenzies. They believed that in this way they were communing with the divine.

In Corinth, it seems that some of the pagan practices were being incorporated into the exercise of some of the gifts of the Spirit. The believers there were not so much interested in serving, learning, and edifying. Instead, they seemed to compete for attention and self-glory by the way they distorted the use of languages.

1. The Superiority of Prophecy over Tongues (14:1-6)

One of the questions that must be answered very early in our study of 1 Corinthians 14 is this: Were tongues *known languages*, or was the phenomenon some sort of frenzied *ecstatic speech*?

The manifestation of tongues in Acts 2 (on the Day of Pentecost) involved known languages. The miracle at Pentecost was the fact that those who spoke, *spoke in existing languages* which they never before used. Some believe that the nature of the tongues evident in Acts *was different from* the tongues referred to in the church at Corinth. There are a number of reasons why many Bible students, however, believe that the true gift of tongues referred to in 1 Corinthians 14 was also a reference to *real languages*—but that some in Corinth were turning "tongues" into a kind of trance, and were using some kind of ecstatic utterance as a substitute for the genuine manifestation of tongues.

We must remember that the word "unknown" (used in the KJV, but in italicized form) was not in the original Greek text, and thus it is only the word "tongue" that we find in the original text in 1 Corinthians 14.[82]

Paul told the Christians at Corinth (in 2 Corinthians 8:7) that they abound in knowledge—or as the *Living Bible* paraphrases it, *"You people...have...so much learning."* It was obvious that the Corinthians had much formal training since they could often speak in a foreign language to those who did not understand them in their own language.

The whole point of this chapter in 1 Corinthians is that Paul was seeking to *correct* and *regulate* their use of tongues. He was not exhorting them to exercise the gift.

(14:1) Pursue love, and desire spiritual gifts, but especially that you may prophesy.

The Greek word translated *pursue* is a strenuous word—a word which shows the need for effort and dedication and persistent watching. We are to "pursue" love, set our hearts on manifesting it, and resolve to make love our chief goal in exercising our gifts.

The Greek word translated *desire* (in verse 1, *and in* 1 Corinthians 12:31) means "to show enthusiasm for" the

---

[82] The "tongues" in Isaiah 28:11-12 (and referred to in 1 Corinthians 14:21) *were actual languages* used in Isaiah's time. This is one of several reasons why it is best to interpret the tongues described in 1 Corinthians 14 as being actual languages. Isaiah was announcing that a people (the Assyrians) who spoke another tongue would be conquering Israel. See footnote 84 on page 172.

blessing of spiritual gifts. We are to have *a keen interest in* spiritual gifts, but at no place are we told to go *searching for* spiritual gifts, because each person is given spiritual gifts as the Spirit chooses (1 Corinthians 12:11).

It is true that in 1 Corinthians 12:31 believers are told to "earnestly desire" the best gifts—but the word "desire" used there (Greek, *zeloute*) means "to be zealous of" (to have a keen interest in) the best gifts. The Greek language has words meaning "to seek," but those words are never used to encourage *seeking for* spiritual gifts.

Verse 12 of 1 Corinthians 14 implies that while it is proper *to be zealous about* the use of spiritual gifts, it is much more important that *we seek* to prophesy, and in fact, we should want to "excel" in the use of prophecy. The word "seek" (Greek *zeteite*) is a strong word which means "to *eagerly* desire" to use the gift of prophecy.

All through this section Paul is speaking not to individuals, but to the whole local body. The Greek "you" (which is merely implied at some places) is plural.[83] It is God's will that His people *strive to prophesy, that is, to edify one another*.

(14:2) For he who speaks in a tongue does not speak to men but to God, for no one understands him; however, in the spirit he speaks mysteries.

We must remember (from back in 1 Corinthians 12:10) that *the gift of prophecy* is the Spirit-given ability to proclaim the Word of God with clarity, and to apply it in such a way that it will edify the church. *The gift of tongues* is the gift which enables persons to speak in a natural language even though they never previously learned it.

---

[83] At no place are *individuals* told to personally look for their gifts. The plural "you" means that *the local church as a body* is to desire that the best gifts are manifested in its midst.

The reason why the gift of prophecy is more valuable than the gift of tongues—is that one who speaks in a tongue is speaking in a language unknown to others. The tongues-speaker may indeed be speaking to God and edifying himself, but he is doing nothing to benefit the church, for no one can understand what is being said.

(14:3-4) But he who prophesies speaks edification and exhortation and comfort to men. He who speaks in a tongue edifies himself, but he who prophesies edifies the church.

God has given gifts to believers "for the profit of all" (1 Corinthians 12:7). Those who prophesy build up the larger church, whereas those who speak in a tongue are merely building up themselves as they seek fellowship with God. Prophesying, by way of contrast, brings edification, exhortation, and comfort.

Edification means building up Christian character. *Exhortation* speaks of admonition and encouragement. *Comfort* refers to the act of calming and bringing consolation to those who are hurting. The mother who comforts a restless child during the night-time hours is practicing a form of prophesying.

From the definition in verse 3, we may conclude that prophesying includes *a ministry of strengthening*—it instructs and feeds the soul. It includes *a ministry of stirring*—it awakens and arouses one who has gone to sleep spiritually. It includes *a ministry of soothing*—it does much more than the sign in the novelty shop, which reads, "We mend everything except broken hearts."

(14:5) I wish you all spoke with tongues, but even more that you prophesied; for he who prophesies is greater than he who speaks with tongues, unless indeed he interprets, that the church may receive edification.

Paul had no problem with those who used a special language in their private devotion before God—but in public, prophecy is much better than tongues. If the message in tongues is interpreted (which, from the context, was *not* likely the case)—then to use tongues is acceptable. On the other hand, the greatest task one can perform in the church is the act of prophesying—proclaiming the Word of God with clarity so that others will be edified.

(14:6) But now, brethren, if I come to you speaking with tongues, what shall I profit you unless I speak to you either by revelation, by knowledge, by prophesying, or by teaching?

The church cannot be edified in any profitable way unless the messages that it receives are understandable. Even if Paul himself came and spoke to the people in tongues, it would do them no good because they would not be able to comprehend the meaning of what he was saying.

The terms "revelation, knowledge, prophesying, and teaching" all tend to shade into one another, and it is not necessary to try and establish rigid distinctions between them. Each of the words expresses an attempt to convey truth by means of clear explanations.

2. Limitations on Speaking in Tongues (14:7-25)

No one can communicate God's truth through meaningless sounds. Those who spoke in tongues at Corinth were interested in impressing others, not in communicating God's truth clearly in order to edify.

(14:7-9) Even things without life, whether flute or harp, when they make a sound, unless they make a distinction in the sounds, how will it be known what is piped or played? For if the trumpet makes an uncertain sound, who will prepare for battle? So likewise you, unless you utter

by the tongue words easy to understand, how will it be known what is spoken? For you will be speaking into the air.

We are to aim for clarity and should seek to avoid confusion. Paul uses two examples to illustrate—the first from musical instruments; the other is an example from human languages.

In music, melody and harmony are dependent upon a consistency of tone and rhythm in order to make sensible sounds. Unless the notes given by the flute and harp and trumpet are distinct, and not running confusedly into one another, no one can tell what is being sounded.

It is the same with speech. Unless a person speaks intelligible words with the tongue, how will anyone know what is being said? The phrase "speaking into the air" is a proverbial way of saying the speech is ineffective.

(14:10-12) There are, it may be, so many kinds of languages in the world, and none of them is without significance. Therefore, if I do not know the meaning of the language, I shall be a foreigner to him who speaks, and he who speaks will be a foreigner to me. Even so you, since you are zealous for spiritual gifts, let it be for the edification of the church that you seek to excel.

The second illustration is taken from the use of many different languages. No communication results if people are speaking two or more different languages. Just so, in Corinth, lots of noise was creating nothing but chaos in their worship services.

The word "foreigner" (Greek, *barbaros*) came to be applied to all who did not speak Greek. The word validates the conclusion that in 1 Corinthians 14 Paul has in mind *known foreign languages* when he talks about tongues.

In verse 12 we are reminded that the primary aim of the exercise of the gift of tongues is to "let it be for the edification of the church."

(14:13-14) Therefore let him who speaks in a tongue pray that he may interpret. For if I pray in a tongue, my spirit prays, but my understanding is unfruitful.

The people at Corinth were not asked to give up their use of tongues, but they were encouraged to pray for good ability to interpret what was spoken in a language not known by some who heard the message.

The word "spirit" (used in verses 14-15) does not refer to the Holy Spirit, but to the inner person (as in First Corinthians 2:11). If one who speaks is to edify others, he must himself understand what he is saying.

(14:15-17) What is the conclusion then? I will pray with the spirit, and I will also pray with the understanding. I will sing with the spirit, and I will also sing with the understanding. Otherwise, if you bless with the spirit, how will he who occupies the place of the uninformed say "Amen" at your giving of thanks, since he does not understand what you say? For you indeed give thanks well, but the other is not edified.

When a Christian prays or sings or pronounces a blessing, there must be understanding. If there is no understanding, there is no blessing. How can the ordinary person (one without special training) say "Amen" at the end of a prayer verbalized in tongues, if he does not understand what was said? And so, speaking in tongues is an activity inferior to the gift of prophecy, because tongues are a stumbling block to the uninformed.

(14:18-19) I thank my God I speak with tongues more than you all; yet in the church I would rather speak five words with my understanding, that I may teach others also, than ten thousand words in a tongue.

Paul had the ability to speak in foreign tongues. He was much more skilled in the use of several languages than the folks at Corinth were. Paul was able to speak Hebrew,

Greek, Latin, and Aramaic—but he hastens to add that he would rather speak five words in a language that the people understood so that they might grow spiritually, than to try and impress people with his many languages.

(14:20) Brethren, do not be children in understanding; however, in malice be babes, but in understanding be mature.

The fact that the believers at Corinth used tongues in the form of an ecstatic heavenly language—showed that they were still spiritual children. They had a childish fascination for an activity which appealed to their love for personal display. (Of course, it is not always a negative quality to be like children. To be *childlike*, in soon forgetting little disputes with others, is commendable.)

(14:21) In the law it is written: "With men of other tongues and other lips I will speak to this people; And yet, for all that, they will not hear Me," says the Lord.

Paul uses a quotation from Isaiah 28:11 to show that God intended tongues (a foreign language) to be a sign for unbelievers. Isaiah the prophet told the people of Judah that if they refused to listen to the plain words that he was using about coming judgment, God would speak to them through the lips of foreigners[84] in a language the Jews did not understand. Israel paid no attention to Isaiah, and so when the invading Assyrian army spoke in their own language in the midst of Judah—that strange tongue was a reminder to the Jews of God's judgment.

(14:22) Therefore tongues are for a sign, not to those who believe but to unbelievers; but prophesying is not for unbelievers but for those who believe.

---

[84] This illustration clearly indicates again that the "tongues" Paul is talking about in 1 Corinthians 14 is a reference to foreign languages rather than ecstatic utterances. See also footnote 82 on page 166.

The point is that *since God intended tongues to be a sign to unbelievers*, the Corinthians should not be putting so much emphasis on tongues in their assemblies of Christians. It would be better to focus on prophecy—the simple proclamation of God's Word in order to strengthen the believers.

(14:23-25) Therefore if the whole church comes together in one place, and all speak with tongues, and there come in those who are uninformed or unbelievers, will they not say that you are out of your mind? But if all prophesy, and an unbeliever or an uninformed person comes in, he is convinced by all, he is convicted by all. And thus the secrets of his heart are revealed; and so, falling down on his face, he will worship God and report that God is truly among you.

Paul, in this passage, describes the differing effects of tongues and prophecy on outsiders. It is clear that prophecy is superior to the use of tongues in providing help for unbelievers.

Paul concludes this section on the *limitations* of speaking in tongues, by saying that if the entire church conducts a meeting *in tongues (strange languages)*—and "unbelievers" (or basically "uninformed" persons) enter the service—they will say that these people are out of their minds, and will be repelled by the apparent confusion.

On the other hand, if folks enter the service and they hear *a message proclaimed with understandable and clear words* (prophecy), they will find the inner thoughts of their hearts exposed, and will more likely be convinced of the truth, and compelled to confess that God is present in the meeting and that He has spoken to them.

Because the Word of God *presented in plain speech* is the means by which unbelievers are converted, and the means by which those who have believed are nurtured—it is important to limit the use of tongues in worship services, and instead, emphasize the clear presentation of Bible messages in a language that the audience can understand.

3. Regulations for Worship in the Church (14:26-40)

Paul had stressed the importance of focusing on the use of the gift of prophecy in the church. Now he cites the need for order in the worship services when God's people assemble together.

Evidently there was a great deal of confusion in the services held at Corinth. One person wanted to sing a psalm, another wanted to exercise the gift of prophecy, and still another wanted to speak in a tongue.

The first and last verses of this section contain words that are the key to understanding the thought. At the end of verse 26, we read, "Let all things be done for edification." And verse 40 says, "Let all things be done decently and in order."

(14:26) How is it then, brethren? Whenever you come together, each of you has a psalm, has a teaching, has a tongue, has a revelation, has an interpretation. Let all things be done for edification.

Worship services in the early church often consisted of several parts. Each member was allowed to participate. One person would want to sing a psalm; another would be led to explain a Bible doctrine; a third person might want to offer a testimony (even in a language not known by the entire audience). There had to be some kind of order so that the presentations would be up-building to those present. Each presenter needed to exercise self-control and respect for the others who had part in the service.

(14:27-28) If anyone speaks in a tongue, let there be two or at the most three, each in turn, and let one interpret. But if there is no interpreter, let him keep silent in church, and let him speak to himself and to God.

One regulation was that only two (or at most three) persons were allowed to speak in any one service.[85] They were to speak one at a time, and with someone interpreting if the presentation involves tongues. If there was no interpreter, then the speaker was to be silent in the church service, and speak only to himself and to God.

(14:29-30) Let two or three prophets speak, and let the others judge. But if anything is revealed to another who sits by, let the first keep silent.

If while one person was speaking, God gave to another believer a special deep insight into the Scriptures, the first speaker was to be silent while the new revelation was shared with the audience. Other persons were to "judge" (Greek, *diakrinetosan*), meaning "to discern and evaluate what was said."

(14:31-33) For you can all prophesy one by one, that all may learn and all may be encouraged. And the spirits of the prophets are subject to the prophets. For God is not the author of confusion but of peace, as in all the churches of the saints.

Except for the matter of interpretation, the same rules applied also to the exercise of the gift of prophecy. Those who were called to prophesy were to speak one by one in an orderly fashion. Each speaker was to exercise self-control so that there would be sufficient time for the other speakers.

---

[85] William Barclay says, "Clearly the early church had no professional ministry." He asks, "Has the church done rightly or wrongly in instituting a professional ministry?" Barclay acknowledges that there is some value in having ministers set apart to live close to God and to bring his fellow men the truth and comfort they need, "But on the other hand there is the obvious danger that when a man becomes a professional preacher he is at least sometimes in the position of having to say something when he has really nothing to say…it is certainly a mistake to think that only the professional ministry can ever bring God's truth to men" (*The Letters to the Corinthians*, page 149-150).

Sometimes preachers of the Word need to share the service with other speakers who don't know when to stop, and that can be very discouraging. One such inconsiderate speaker claimed that when the Holy Spirit takes over in his delivery, he cannot be troubled by watching a clock! Paul's argument in these verses is that the spiritual gifts are to be exercised in an orderly fashion.

The purpose for gathering in an assembled meeting is so that *"all may learn and all may be encouraged"* (verse 31b). Every church service should be a learning experience. The Word of God never changes but it needs to be carefully expounded and applied to the constantly changing situations of life.

Verse 32 says that "the spirits of the prophets are subject to the prophets"—that is, even true preachers of the Word don't know everything, and thus when a prophetic utterance is given, it is "subject" (Greek, *hupotasso*) to being checked by others[86] who have the gift of prophecy.

God is not a God of confusion and disorder (verse 33), but a God of peace and One who loves harmony.

In the section that follows (verses 34-35) Paul turns to the role of women in public worship. The latter part of verse 33 states clearly that what is instructed here is the same as what has been addressed everywhere "in all the churches of the saints."

(14:34-35) Let your women keep silent in the churches, for they are not permitted to speak; but they are to

---

[86] Early Brethren in the plural "free ministry" system generally had at least one additional minister bear testimony to the words which had just been spoken in the prophetic utterance. This is still practiced among the free ministry churches. Carl F. Bowman says that preaching usually covered a chapter of the New Testament "followed up by remarks from additional ministers"—which later "gave way to sermons that were planned in advance by a single minister on a theme of his choice" (*Brethren Society*, page 148).

be submissive, as the law also says. And if they want to learn something, let them ask their own husbands at home; for it is shameful for women to speak in church.

The essence of the instruction is that women are to remain silent in the churches (the assemblies of gathered believers). They are not to speak, but are to be in submission, "as the law also says."[87] They are, in fact, not even to ask questions in the Christian assembly, but are to "ask their own husbands at home."

The word "silent" is qualified by the context of the passage. Corinthian services were a noisy and discordant scene. The word "speak" (Greek, *laleo*) refers to *"talking, chattering, questioning, arguing"*—a direct reference to disruptive behavior.[88] And so the prohibition is related especially to the particular problem of disorder in the worship services. Sisters in an assembly of God's people must guard against disruptive behavior.

In light of the context, the silence mandated (in verse 34a) is not a reference to *absolute* silence. It does not mean that women may not sing or read Bible verses or whisper to a child in an attempt to discipline, and the like.

The text says that it is "shameful" for a woman to speak in a gathered assembly. That is, the woman's station in life requires modesty, humility, and quiet submission to the leadership of man. Thus women should not be so bold as to want to take part in the public services of teaching and having oversight of congregations. What is said here should

---

[87] A reference to Genesis 3:16. One of the consequences of the Fall was that the woman's "desire shall be for your husband, and he shall rule over you."

[88] All wanted to exercise their gifts, and all would speak at once. Whatever else the restriction here may imply, it certainly means that women were not to interrupt with controversial questions in the church service. Most women in New Testament times did not have formal schooling, and so they were especially inclined to be inquisitive.

also be compared with 1 Timothy 2:11-15 where it is stated that women are designed by the Creator to train godly offspring.[89] They are neither to teach men nor to "have" (*take a position of*) authority over them.

There are many ministries which godly women can perform; however, the role of the Christian woman is primarily a quiet ministry, giving help to a variety of persons in need:

One ministry is *to teach* children and younger women (Titus 2:4). Many women have demonstrated their ability to accomplish these tasks very well.

Another ministry is to *show kindness* to her family of children in the home. The mother who carefully instructs her children is molding the thinking of future generations; she has within her reach the power of shaping the world through the influence of a godly home.

J. Allen Blair tells of a woman who had recently been converted. She suffered a considerable amount of antagonism from her husband. Blair describes the situation: "When your husband is angry and unkind, what do you do?" a friend asked. "I cook his food better," she replied. "When he complains, I sweep the floor cleaner. And when he speaks sharply I answer him mildly. I try to show him that when I became a Christian, I became a better wife and

---

[89] Women were widely used in many capacities in the early church, but we find no evidence that they served in *positions of leadership* and *teachers of doctrinal truth* in the assembly. The *daughters of Philip* "prophesied" (Acts 21:9)—but there is no record that they did so in a mixed church congregation. *Mothers and grandmothers* taught children spiritual truth (2 Timothy 3:14-15), but that was quite different from conducting a worship service in the church. *Priscilla joined her husband* in giving instructions to Apollos (Acts 18:26), but that was in private. *Positions* of leadership in the church were filled by Christian men. There are times when men and women meet informally in Bible studies where *all* might share questions and insights—but when the church comes together as a body, leadership is reserved for men.

a better mother." Blair continues, "This husband could stand all the preaching from the pulpit, but he could not stand [his wife's] practical Christian living. Soon he gave his heart to God." In a final comment he says that Paul knew that if women "were doing what they should be doing in the home they would have little time to preach. The preaching was to be left to the men" (*Living Wisely: A Devotional Study of the First Epistle to the Corinthians*, page 296).

Also, women *may pray*. There were women among the disciples waiting in the upper room for the promise of the Holy Spirit during the days leading up to Pentecost. Acts 1:14 says that *all* those disciples "continued...in prayer and supplication, with the women." In Acts 12:5, the entire church was in constant prayer for Peter's welfare.

A fourth activity for women is to *minister to those in need* during times of sickness. In Romans 16:1-2 we read about Phoebe who comforted the sad, and lifted the spirits of those who were discouraged. Many times women need special help of the kind that only another woman can appropriately give—counsel and help related to child birth, miscarriages, mastectomies, menopause, and so forth.

(14:36) Or did the word of God come originally from you? Or was it you only that it reached?

Many irregularities had taken place in the church at Corinth, including women discarding the head veil. Some abused the lovefeast; others misused spiritual gifts; some women spoke out in the worship services, and so forth. It seems that some of the believers contended with Paul about these matters. They wanted to follow their own standards regardless of what Paul or the other apostles said.

By maintaining this attitude, some at Corinth were putting themselves above the Scriptures. So Paul challenges them with biting words: "Did the word of God come originally from you?" In essence, the believers at Corinth were told that faithful children of God are to obey the Word which has *come from God*. We are to abide by *His* rules.

(14:37) If anyone thinks himself to be a prophet or spiritual, let him acknowledge that the things which I write to you are the commandments of the Lord.

Everything Paul taught about God and the gospel came from God. If there are those who profess to be spiritual and to have the gift of prophecy, they must recognize that the commandments uttered by Paul are given in the name of (and by the authority of) the Lord.

Paul insists that the things he has written to the Corinthians are "the commandments of the Lord." His writing was not tainted by cultural or personal bias as some critics claim. What is said in Paul's writings is the inspired Word of God. Paul himself did not give us the teaching found in his epistles. God gave it. The Apostle was simply the medium through whom God spoke.

(14:38) But if anyone is ignorant, let him be ignorant.

That is, Paul will not argue with him; he will simply let the individual continue in his ignorance.

Those who do not recognize Paul's authority will refuse his words at their own peril. Paul delivered the commands of God, and those who disregard them, and doubt whether they were given by divine authority, are really rejecting the law of God!

(14:39) Therefore, brethren, desire earnestly to prophesy, and do not forbid to speak with tongues.

The whole focus of 1 Corinthians 14 is on the superior value of prophecy—that is, proclaiming God's truth in a clear way using a language that people can understand. The most effective ministry any congregation can have will come from the clear proclamation of the powerful Word of God. The gift of tongues (speaking in a language not natively acquired) may have some value, but it must never be allowed to replace the simple and clear preaching and exposition of the Word.

(14:40) Let all things be done decently and in order.

All activity is to be done properly and in an orderly way. God is not the source of confusion, nor is He pleased with indecency and disorder.

There are a few additional observations about the modern tongues movement:

(1) It is not necessary to try to prove to charismatics that their gifts are not valid; it is better to insist that they confine the exercise of the alleged gift to the regulations and limitations imposed by the Scriptures. These include one speaker at a time (14:27), no women speaking (14:34), no confusion (14:33), and the use of an interpreter (14:28). Some aspects of the modern charismatic movement may be more authentic than critics will acknowledge.

(2) In evaluating the modern "tongues movement," *some* would say it is of the devil. That may be true in some extreme instances. *Others* would say that these are Christians who love the Lord, and the movement is of the Holy Spirit. It is more likely that the ecstatic utterances which lead to unintelligible messages, typical of many charismatic services, are simply of human fleshly origin.[90]

---

[90] The Mennonite writer, Sanford Shetler, says, "It is difficult to understand how it has come about through the years, that a passage of Scripture which so definitely stresses the advantage of prophecy over tongues, should ever have been misconstrued to mean the exact opposite." (*Paul's Letter to the Corinthians,* page 151).

Proclaiming God's Word in an intelligible way is of much greater value, both for the church and for unbelievers, than is any use of tongues—even the true gift of tongues.

Chapter 12

BODILY RESURRECTION
1 Corinthians 15:1-58

Some people at Corinth continued to question the reality of the bodily resurrection. In 1 Corinthians 15 we are given the most extensive treatment of the doctrine of the resurrection that can be found anywhere in Scripture.

Paul begins by explaining that the resurrection is a major part of the gospel message, and then he goes on to give a clear definition of what comprises the gospel. The whole chapter is designed to show that the resurrection is a historical fact, and that it is one of the most important truths of the Christian message.

1. Importance of the Resurrection (15:1-19)

The Greeks believed that when death came, the *body* was laid away in the tomb and that was the end of it. Marcus Aurelius said, "When a man dies, all that is left is dust, ashes, bones, and stench." They did believe, however, that the *soul* lives on in an after-world.

(15:1-2) Moreover, brethren, I declare to you the gospel which I preached to you, which also you received and in which you stand, by which also you are saved, if you hold fast that word which I preached to you—unless you believed in vain.

Paul presents the resurrection as one of the core teachings of the gospel. Without the resurrection there is no Christianity.

The phrase *"if you hold fast that word which I preached to you"*—reminds us that the proof of our true reception of the gospel is to continue in the faith. When we decide for Christ and receive water baptism and become a member of a local church—that step is only the beginning of the Christian life.

The words *"unless you believed in vain"* are a reminder that our earlier commitments to Christ will not benefit us if we do not *continue* in the faith.

(15:3-5) For I delivered to you first of all that which I also received: that Christ died for our sins according to the Scriptures, and that He was buried, and that He rose again the third day according to the Scriptures, and that He was seen by Cephas, then by the twelve.

In this section Paul names the essentials of the gospel. He presents four historical facts which are basic to the gospel, each beginning with the word "that."

"Christ died for our sins according to the Scriptures." The death of Christ was not an after-thought with God. It had been planned and prophesied many years before the event took place. See the Scripture accounts in Psalm 22 and Isaiah 53.

"He was buried." The burial was necessary to set the stage for the resurrection. (We prefer to bury, rather than cremate our dead, merely to follow Jesus' example.)

"He arose again the third day according to the Scriptures." The verb "arose" (Greek, *egegertai*) is in the perfect tense, meaning that He arose, and He is still alive!

"He was seen by Cephas, then by the twelve." This fact confirms the third fact. Jesus was seen after the resurrection. Christ's life after death is not a false claim which cannot be verified.

(15:6-8) After that He was seen by over five hundred brethren at once, of whom the greater part remain to the present, but some have fallen asleep. After that He was seen by James, then by all the apostles. Then last of all He was seen by me also, as by one born out of due time.

Paul names some of those who saw the Lord Jesus after His resurrection. He appeared to Peter (*Cephas* was his Aramaic name), and then to the rest of the disciples (verse 5), and then to five hundred "brethren" (verse 6), and to James (verse 7) most likely the half-brother of Jesus, and one who did not believe in Jesus as the Messiah during our Lord's earthly ministry (John 7:5).

In verse 8 Paul describes his coming to faith as "one born out of due time." His conversion on the Damascus Road came later than that of the other apostles, and he was suddenly thrust into the apostleship. It was the bright light and the voice from heaven during the Damascus Road experience that convinced Paul that Jesus really was alive.

(15:9-11) For I am the least of the apostles, who am not worthy to be called an apostle, because I persecuted the church of God. But by the grace of God I am what I am, and His grace toward me was not in vain; but I labored more abundantly than they all, yet not I, but the grace of God which was with me. Therefore, whether it was I or they, so we preach and so you believed.

Paul considers himself the least of the apostles because at one time he had bitterly persecuted the church. That was an enormous crime and he did not feel worthy to be called an apostle. Paul acknowledged that it was God's unmerited favor that enabled him to perform a worthwhile ministry for Christ.

In verse 11 Paul says that whether it was he (or any of the other apostles) who preached, they were all united in their testimony about the gospel, and about the doctrine of the resurrection in particular.

(15:12-13) Now if Christ is preached that He has been raised from the dead, how do some among you say that there is no resurrection of the dead? But if there is no resurrection of the dead, then Christ is not risen.

Some in Corinth were denying that any kind of resurrection of the body was possible. To the Greeks, *the body* was the source of a human being's weakness and sin and death. Resurrecting the body, then, would only enslave the soul again. But the evidence was clear. Paul had just shown that the resurrection of Christ is a historical fact. If bodily resurrection is not possible, then Christ Himself has not risen from the dead, or as the Moffatt translation says it, "Then even Christ did not rise."

(15:14-16) And if Christ is not risen, then our preaching is empty and your faith is also empty. Yes, and we are found false witnesses of God, because we have testified of God that He raised up Christ, whom He did not raise up—if in fact the dead do not rise. For if the dead do not rise, then Christ is not risen.

If Christ did not rise, then the whole gospel message crumbles in the dust. If the bodily resurrection of Jesus is not true, then preaching that He has been raised from the dead is empty and meaningless. And our faith in Christ (Who was supposed to have been raised from the dead) is also without meaning and value.

Paul repeats the statement made earlier—that if the dead do not rise, then Christ did not rise either (verse 16).

(15:17-19) And if Christ is not risen, your faith is futile; you are still in your sins! Then also those who have fallen asleep in Christ have perished. If in this life only we have hope in Christ, we are of all men the most pitiable.

If Christ did not rise, then faith in Him as our Savior is meaningless—and we still carry the guilt of our sins. We could not be justified and ready for Heaven.

Our own future is dependent upon Christ's bodily resurrection. If Christ did not rise, then our loved ones who have died in Christ before us have perished without hope. Our loved ones would be gone from us forever! The dying

Christian would have to hold out his cold trembling hand, and grasp the hand of the wife who traveled by his side, and say, "Farewell forever, my good wife, farewell." Those whom we loved dearly, we will never see again and we ourselves are to be pitied. Or, as some translations render it, we would be "the most miserable of creatures."

By way of contrast to this hopelessness, the Bible teaches that upon death, the physical body rests in the place of burial, but the spirits of the saints go to be with the Lord and exist in a state of bliss (2 Corinthians 5:8). And there will be a future resurrection.

Paul's argument for the necessity of Christ's resurrection cannot be disputed. If Christ arose, the Christian faith is real; if He did not rise, our faith means nothing. If the Christian hope does not benefit us beyond the grave, we have nothing toward which to look forward, and our supposed salvation is meaningless.

2. The Order of Future Resurrections (15:20-34)

The resurrection of Christ did occur and is a guarantee of more resurrections still to come. Paul uses two illustrations in verses 20-21 to show the relationship between Christ's resurrection and ours.

(15:20) But now Christ is risen from the dead, and has become the firstfruits of those who have fallen asleep.

Praise God! Jesus did rise! And there were many eyewitnesses to His resurrected Presence!

Paul explains in verse 20 that even though up to the present no human ever returned from the dead in a new body—the resurrection of Christ is a guarantee that more resurrections are still to come. Jesus became "the firstfruits of those who have fallen asleep"—and every Israelite knew what the "firstfruits" were.

In Old Testament times, in the late spring of the year, the first sheaf of newly ripened grain was taken to the tabernacle and laid on the altar. It was offered *as a pledge* that the whole coming harvest would be dedicated to the Lord. The presentation of the firstfruits was always done on a Sunday, the day after the Sabbath (Leviticus 23:10-11).

That event was known as the Feast of Firstfruits—and now Paul says that the resurrection of Christ is like those first sheaves of grain brought to the tabernacle. His resurrection is a pledge (a guarantee) that a vast harvest of human bodies will still be resurrected in the future.[91]

(15:21-22) For since by man came death, by Man also came the resurrection of the dead. For as in Adam all die, even so in Christ all shall be made alive.

Adam sinned in the Garden of Eden and *all who were in Adam* (that is, the whole human race) died. But it is also true that *all who are in Christ* (that is, those "in Christ") will be made alive. The act of one man affected all in his group. The *first* man, Adam, transgressed God's law and brought sin and death into the world (Genesis 3:17-24; Romans 5:12-19). The *second* Man, Jesus Christ, was the perfect sacrifice to take away sin and to bring life to those who believe in Him (Romans 5:15-21).

Then in verses 23-28, we learn about the order of those future resurrections.

(15:23) But each one in his own order: Christ the firstfruits, afterward those who are Christ's at His coming.

---

[91] Human beings do not ordinarily return from the dead to tell what the afterworld is like. Harry Houdini was an escapist magician. He was buried in sealed coffins, sewed into canvas bags, locked in guarded jail cells, stuffed in milk cans, riveted into boilers—but always moments later, Houdini would appear in the presence of his audience again. Houdini died on October 31, 1926, and promised that he would return if at all possible. Séances were held every year for many years on October 31, but Houdini never appeared.

All human beings will be resurrected, but not all at the same time.[92] Paul wanted to clarify that there is an order to the resurrections.

In Luke 14, Jesus spoke about those who invite the poor and deprived to a feast in their homes, and says, "You shall be repaid *at the resurrection of the just*" (verse 14). The *first* resurrection of human beings does not include all who have died, but only those who have died with faith in Jesus Christ.

Jesus was the first to rise from the dead (Acts 26:23). Afterward, "those who are Christ's" shall be raised "at His coming" (1 Thessalonians 4:13-18).

(15:24-26) Then comes the end, when He delivers the kingdom to God the Father, when He puts an end to all rule and all authority and power. For He must reign till He has put all enemies under His feet. The last enemy that will be destroyed is death.

Some day the end will come. In these verses Paul describes in a general way some of the final events which will take place before eternity will be ushered in.

Only one more class of the dead remains to be resurrected—the unsaved and lost, those who rejected Christ. At some unspecified time, in connection with His second coming, the resurrected Christ will conquer all evil, and destroy those enemies that oppose God.

Paul looks to the end of the millennial reign of Christ on the earth when all human history will be concluded. At that time Christ will deliver up the kingdom to the Father, and He will even abolish the last enemy—

---

[92] Jesus clearly declared that "the hour is coming in which all who are in the graves will hear His voice and come forth—those who have done good to the resurrection of life, and those who have done evil, to the resurrection of condemnation" (John 5:28-29).

death. Death will be banished forever. Verse 25 says that "He must reign"—meaning that He will definitely (without a doubt) reign as the ultimate Ruler.

We are told in Revelation 20:4-5, after describing the first resurrection, that "the rest of the dead did not live again until the thousand years were finished."[93]

(15:27-28) For "He has put all things under His feet." But when He says "all things are put under Him," it is evident that He who put all things under Him is excepted. Now when all things are made subject to Him, then the Son Himself will also be subject to Him who put all things under Him, that God may be all in all.

There are different beliefs about the nature of Christ's "kingdom" (verse 24). Some view the kingdom as a reference to Christ's present rule in the hearts of born again human beings. Others see it as representing the church. The most likely view, in light of the context of this passage, is that it refers to the future reign of Christ on earth.

According to Revelation 20:1-10, Jesus will return and reign on the earth for a period of a thousand years. During that period, righteousness will cover the earth from one end to the other, as the waters cover the sea. Habakkuk 2:14 says that "the earth *will be filled* with the knowledge of the glory of the Lord."

In some final day Christ will voluntarily relinquish His millennial rule to the Father, and God will "be all in all." In Ephesians 1:10-11a, we are told that "in the dispensation of the fullness of the times He might gather

---

[93] The sentence quoted here from Revelation 20:5a is a parenthetical statement. The brief last sentence of verse 5 in Revelation 20 refers back to verse 4 of the same chapter. It will help in understanding Revelation 20:4-6, if the reader will put parentheses around ("But the rest of the dead did not live again until the thousand years were finished"). The parenthetical statement is really an introduction to verse 6.

together in one all things in Christ, both which are in heaven and which are on earth—in Him, in whom also we have obtained an inheritance."

(15:29) Otherwise, what will they do who are baptized for the dead, if the dead do not rise at all? Why then are they baptized for the dead?

A number of explanations have been proposed for this verse. Some (such as the Mormons) actually believe that one can literally be baptized in order to achieve the salvation of other persons. One wealthy woman in Salt Lake City has been baptized 30,000 times for unbaptized dead persons. She paid a sum of money to the church, and was baptized for men like Nebuchadnezzar, Julius Caesar, and Napoleon Bonaparte.

The most simple explanation for verse 29 is to remember that the word "*for* the dead" can easily be translated "*in the place of*" those who have died. In other words, why should a new generation of Christians come along and *fill up the places made vacant* by those who have lived and died during past generations—if there is no resurrection of the dead? Why should we keep on baptizing new converts to the faith—if there is no life beyond the grave anyhow?

(15:30-32) And why do we stand in jeopardy every hour? I affirm, by the boasting in you which I have in Christ Jesus our Lord, I die daily. If, in the manner of men, I have fought with beasts at Ephesus, what advantage is it to me? If the dead do not rise, "Let us eat and drink, for tomorrow we die."

The word "jeopardy" means *danger*, *peril*, or *risk*. Paul was risking his life every hour because there were enemies of Christ lurking in every community. But if there is no resurrection; if there is no hope beyond this life—

what is the sense of putting oneself in the place of danger for the cause of Christ?

The sentence, "I die daily" is most meaningful when translated *"I face death every day of my life"* (Phillips).

It is helpful here to recall the angry mob that pressed upon Paul at Ephesus, as the crowd filled with wrath, shouted, "Great is Diana of the Ephesians!" (Acts 19:28). Because Paul said the pagan gods were not real gods, and instead preached the gospel of Jesus Christ, he was persecuted by a beastly crowd.

Paul's argument is this: Why give up the world and live a life of self-denial for the cause of Christ—if the dead do not rise?[94] Why not try to get all the enjoyment out of this world that one can get?

(15:33-34) Do not be deceived: "Evil company corrupts good habits." Awake to righteousness, and do not sin; for some do not have the knowledge of God. I speak this to your shame.

We are warned to be careful about the kinds of company we keep. In the first Psalm we are told "not to walk in the counsel of the ungodly, nor to stand in the path of sinners, nor to sit in the seat of the scornful" (Psalm 1:1).

The *ungodly* are not necessarily brazenly wicked persons. They may be nice people, but they have no serious regard for God and for His commandments. The *sinners* are those who rebel against God and are determined to live in sin. They openly revolt against the Lord and defy God's laws. The *scornful* are those who put themselves above

---

[94] The Brethren writer, L. W. Teeter, comments on these verses: "If there is no resurrection, there is no use in being exposed continually to persecutions and death in order to attain to a resurrection....[the words] *I die daily* mean I am daily exposed to danger and death" (*New Testament Commentary*, pages 145-146, published by Brethren Publishing House in 1894).

God—people who are arrogant and quarrelsome, quick to ridicule and sneer at God.

God's people are not to linger and loiter with such persons. We will seek to win sinners to faith in Christ, and thus we will mingle with them—but we will not spend long hours finding satisfaction and fellowship with those who defy God's laws. Instead, we will seek to live by the laws of God, and be alert to those things which are righteous according to His standards.

3. The Nature of the Resurrection Body (15:35-50)

In this section the question is asked, "How are the dead raised up? And with what body do they come?"

Most of us are curious, and we wonder how will these resurrections take place? We wonder what will our new resurrected bodies be like? These questions are answered in verses 36-41.

(15:35-38) But someone will say, "How are the dead raised up? And with what body do they come?" Foolish one, what you sow is not made alive unless it dies. And what you sow, you do not sow that body that shall be, but mere grain—perhaps wheat or some other grain. But God gives it a body as He pleases, and to each seed its own body.

In verses 36-38 Paul speaks about plant life. Seeds are sown into the soil, and later they die. They decay in the ground—but in doing so, the tiny seed sends forth a new plant. The plant looks different from the seed, and yet it has a certain identity with that seed.

A dry, dead-looking seed is placed into the ground, but by God's power, in a brief time a green plant comes up—a plant that is vigorous and beautiful. The plant is a new and different body, yet related to the seed from which it came. And just as we see the power of God at work in our gardens (a dry seed producing a new green plant)—so we must trust the same power of God to be able to give us a new vigorous body in the life to come!

(15:39-41) All flesh is not the same flesh, but there is one kind of flesh of men, another flesh of animals, another of fish, and another of birds. There are also celestial bodies and terrestrial bodies; but the glory of the celestial is one, and the glory of the terrestrial is another. There is one glory of the sun, another glory of the moon, and another glory of the stars; for one star differs from another star in glory.

The differing kinds of bodies that animals and birds and fish have should make it easy for us to believe that God can provide a resurrection body for us—a body that is different from the body which we now have.

Fish have one kind of body; birds have another kind of body; land animals have still another kind of body. Fish are designed for swimming; birds for flying; animals for walking and running. Surely the same Divine Power that gives all kinds of bodies to the animal kingdom can provide another form for our human bodies—a form which is suitable for the environment of Heaven.

Verses 40-41 are a reminder that there is much variety in the universe. There is a difference between celestial [heavenly] bodies (sun, moon, and stars), and the terrestrial [earthly] bodies (trees, canyons, and rivers). The splendor of each of these bodies differs. The waterfalls of Yosemite National Park in California differ from the rolling Badlands of South Dakota. The sun is more brilliant than the light reflected by the moon.

There is variety in nature, and just so, our present bodies and our new resurrected bodies are going to differ. Our new bodies will be linked with the old, and have a certain identity with the old, yet they will be different from our present bodies—just as the seed is different from the plant that grows from it.

(15:42) So also is the resurrection of the dead. The body is sown in corruption, it is raised in incorruption.

The new body will not be subject to decay. It will be imperishable. All of us know that our present bodies are perishable. The average life-span in the United States in 1910 was 47 years; today the average life-expectancy is 77 years. There has been lots of progress in the areas of science and medicine, but the processes of aging and wearing still go on. Our hair gets gray; our eyesight becomes more dim; our minds become less alert; and our memory begins to fail.

The new resurrection body (the house we receive when the present old house[95] wears out) will not be subject to disease and decay. There won't be any need for operations, transplants, and immunizations. The new body will be incorruptible. There will be a permanence about the resurrection body in which lovely things will not cease to be lovely.

(15:43) It is sown in dishonor, it is raised in glory. It is sown in weakness, it is raised in power.

The present body "is sown" (buried) in dishonor; it will be raised in glory. We spend much time caring for the human body, but when the spirit leaves the body, there is not too much that is honorable about it. There is a sense in which a corpse is repulsive. We do not care to keep it too long. In countries with a hot climate the bodies of those who have died are often buried the same day.

---

[95] The Apostle Paul speaks about the human body as a "house" in 2 Corinthians 5:1. He says, "For we know that if our earthly house, this tent, is destroyed, we have a building from God, a house not made with hands, eternal in the heavens."

The custom of having flowers at funerals started not only because flowers are beautiful, but also because the fragrance of the lovely flowers helped to overcome the odor of decay.

The body is buried in dishonor. By way of contrast, the new body (of one who died in Christ) will bear the marks of the glory of Christ. When Jesus returns and the graves are opened, "we shall be like Him, for we shall see Him as He is" (1 John 3:2b).

The Apostle John describes the glory of Christ's resurrection body. His *hair* is white as wool; His *voice* is as the sound of many waters; His *countenance* is shining like the sun (Revelation 1:14-16). Our resurrection bodies will be like that—luminous, shining, dazzling—bright like the sun. The body will be "raised in glory."

The present body is buried "in weakness, it is raised in power" (verse 43b). Our present bodies are frail and weak; our new bodies will be full of strength. Our bodies in this world are subject to illness and pain. We experience the pounding of a headache, the sharpness of a toothache, and the gnawing of arthritis.

In this life, there are those who have withered hands and crippled arms and aching feet. Our present bodies often become tired and exhausted. They need rest and food and medical care. By way of contrast, the resurrection body will have new and wonderful powers, free from the limitations of time and space.

(15:44) It is sown a natural body, it is raised a spiritual body. There is a natural body, and there is a spiritual body.

The present body is an earthly human body; the new body will be a heavenly spiritual body. The earthly body is subject to the physical world. If you jump out of a third-story window, you are going to fall. Gravity will pull, and your body will splatter on the ground below.

The heavenly body, by way of contrast, will be subject to the laws of the spirit-world. It will not be *limited* by space nor *barred* by locks nor *hampered* by distance. The body of Jesus, after His resurrection, was different from and yet similar to His former body. It was different, in that He more frequently entered rooms through closed doors and appeared and vanished at will. It was similar, in the sense that He still ate food, bore the marks of suffering, and even had the same tone of voice. It was only when He called Mary's name (on the morning of the resurrection) that she recognized who He was (John 20:16).

Paul, in Philippians 3:20-21, looks forward to the second coming of Jesus, and in essence says that our citizenship is in heaven, from which we also eagerly wait for the Savior, the Lord Jesus Christ, *who will transform our lowly bodies*[96] *that they may be conformed to His glorious body* by the same power which He will use to conquer all else everywhere.

(15:45-49) And so it is written, "The first man Adam became a living being." The last Adam became a life-giving spirit. However, the spiritual is not first, but the natural, and afterward the spiritual. The first man was of the earth, made of dust; the second Man is the Lord from heaven. As was the man of dust, so also are those who are made of dust; and as is the heavenly Man, so also are those who are heavenly. And as we have borne the image of the man of dust, we shall also bear the image of the heavenly Man.

---

[96] On the tombstone of Benjamin Franklin, the printer, are carved the words of the following epitaph: "Here lies the body of Benjamin Franklin, like the cover of an old book, with its contents torn out and stripped of its pages. But it will appear once again in a new and more elegant edition, revised and corrected by the Author."

In this passage there is a distinction between the natural body and the spiritual body. Adam (the first man) and his descendants are contrasted with Christ (the last Adam) and His redeemed ones.

The "natural body" (verse 44b) is a body such as Adam had when he was made from the dust of the ground and given the breath of life (verse 47). The "spiritual body" is the imperishable body that is received from Christ who "became a life-giving spirit" (verse 45b) and which some day will be glorified in Heaven.

(15:50) Now this I say, brethren, that flesh and blood cannot inherit the kingdom of God; nor does corruption inherit incorruption.

It is obvious that our earthly bodies of flesh and blood cannot enter Heaven because our earthly bodies are corruptible. A change must occur, and Paul describes that change in the next section of chapter 15.

4. The Bodies of the Transformed Living (15:51-58)

When Jesus returns to receive the church into His presence, the "dead in Christ" will be raised; we will not all sleep (in death); living believers will be changed; it will happen instantaneously—in the "twinkling of an eye."

(15:51-53) Behold, I tell you a mystery: We shall not all sleep, but we shall all be changed—in a moment, in the twinkling of an eye, at the last trumpet. For the trumpet will sound, and the dead will be raised incorruptible, and we shall be changed. For this corruptible must put on incorruption, and this mortal must put on immortality.

The Lord has chosen not to give any helpful details about the nature of the bodies of *the unsaved dead*, although they too will be raised (John 5:28-29). It is assumed that the unsaved will have throughout eternity the same bodies in which they lived and died in this life—and thus their bodies will not be free from suffering, just as they endured pains and ills in life here on earth.

The words in verses 51-53, by way of contrast, unfold the great truth that not all believers will die in the flesh. Some of God's people will remain alive until the coming of our Lord Jesus. Living Christians will be caught up into the clouds, and they will be miraculously changed. In earlier times this truth had not been revealed.

The bodies of believing Christians will lie in the grave to wait the day of resurrection. The spirit of the individual will, at death, go to be with Jesus in the eternal world (2 Corinthians 5:8). The spirit is alive and will await reunion with the resurrected body. This end-time event is described in more detail in the passage on the Lord's return found in 1 Thessalonians 4:13-18.

(15:54-55) So when this corruptible has put on incorruption, and this mortal has put on immortality, then shall be brought to pass the saying that is written: "Death is swallowed up in victory. O Death, where is your sting? O Hades, where is your victory?"

The term "corruptible" refers to *the dead* whose bodies have corrupted away. The term "mortal" speaks of those who *are living*, but are subject to death. God will take "this corruptible body" and fashion it like unto His own body in glory. The reference to "the saying that is written" is a re-wording of the passage in Isaiah 25:8, and the words "Death is swallowed up in victory" will be explained in the verses that follow.

The questions, "O death, where is your sting?" and "Where is your victory?" are loose translations of a passage in Hosea 13:14. Looking back at Jesus' triumph over death, and forward to the resurrection of the saved followers of Christ—Paul bursts forth in a doxology of praise to God.

The point is clear. Because *our resurrected bodies will be immortal and non-perishable, death will not affect them.* Death will not be able to destroy our resurrection bodies. Instead, in the world to come, the saved will live eternally, free from concerns about death. Paul's confident hope in the future resurrection removes an element of fear that often accompanies thoughts of death.

What is "the sting" of death? It is to come to the end, and to know for an absolute certainty that we have missed it. It is to know that there will never be another chance, and that *if* we had it to do over again, we would live differently. It is to know that time has run out, and now it is too late to undo what was carelessly done.

(15:56-57) The sting of death is sin, and the strength of sin is the law. But thanks be to God, who gives us the victory through our Lord Jesus Christ.

Verse 56 states the relationship between sin, the law, and death. The law declares what is sin, and the wages of sin is death. The knowledge of sin comes through the law, and sin leads to death. But there is hope!

Verse 57 is an appropriate climax to the long discourse on the teaching about the resurrection. There is victory through the Lord Jesus Christ. Because of our embracing the death of Jesus, forgiveness for the believer is an accomplished fact, but the ultimate victory over death comes not because Jesus died, but because He was raised from the dead. And because as Christians we are united to Christ, we shall be resurrected like He was.

The changed bodies of those who have been redeemed (which then will be re-united with the departed spirits)—will experience *plenty* without want, *health* without sickness, *day* without night, *pleasure* without pain, and *life* without death!

(15:58) Therefore, my beloved brethren, be steadfast, immovable, always abounding in the work of the Lord, knowing that your labor is not in vain in the Lord.

The promise of resurrection should have a practical application in our daily lives. Therefore—because all this is true and there *is* life hereafter, we must constantly aim to live our lives here on earth in obedience to God—and in ways that are pleasing to Him.

We are to be "steadfast"—that is, we are to aim to be faithful, *sticking to the task* of building character, and doing the work we are called to do.

We are also to be "immovable"—that is, we are not to be quickly swayed by false teachings which seem to abound everywhere.

The word "always" speaks of continuing effort. The word "abounding" has reference to doing that which is even above the call of duty. It includes the idea of seeking to excel in the Lord's work.

The need for such excellence in our daily labors for Christ cannot be exaggerated. The life of John Wesley provides a good example of abounding in the work of the Lord. For 54 years he preached an average of three sermons a day along with traveling up to twenty miles by horseback. He wrote more than twenty books and edited a set of fifty volumes known as *The Christian Library*. He arose at 4 o'clock in the morning and often labored until 10 o'clock at night. Wesley crowded enormous amounts of work into his lifetime because he was motivated by a keen love for Jesus and for the souls of lost humanity.

There is a sign at the entrance of one of the great manufacturing plants in America that reads: *"If you are like a wheelbarrow, going no farther than pushed—you need not apply for work here."* In the spiritual realm—in light of the promise of a coming resurrection and our ultimate triumph in Christ—we *are to abound* in the Lord's work.

All human beings will be resurrected—no matter what kind of death they have died, or how their bodies were disposed of after death.

Pyramids of granite and marble will be rent in two to let the rising bodies come forth. Mummies will throw off the trappings of centuries. Indian boys (who once played over the hills and valleys of America) will leap from the dust of our streets. The dead of all ages will rise even if their bones lie on some desert wasteland, or at some place on the frozen tundra. The ocean will swell and heave with teaming millions. Those bodies that were cremated and the dust scattered, will come forth. No wonder the Apostle John cried out, "Blessed and holy is he who has part in the first resurrection" (Revelation 20:6a). For those who experience the second death it will be a sad day.

Chapter 13

CONCLUSION: PERSONAL MATTERS
1 Corinthians 16:1-24

In the final chapter of 1 Corinthians, Paul discusses some practical matters. He shifts from emphasizing the glory of the resurrection to the more mundane task of taking an offering for the needs of the church in Jerusalem.

1. Collection for the Poor in Jerusalem (16:1-4)

Paul was accustomed to working with his own hands so that he would not place an undue burden on the churches. On the other hand, he felt free to call upon believers to give generously to support others in need.

(16:1) Now concerning the collection for the saints, as I have given orders to the churches of Galatia, so you must do also:

The words "now concerning" may suggest that the Corinthians had asked Paul about the matter of collecting money for those who were in need. Paul mentions the need of the Christians at Jerusalem.

There may have been a number of reasons why the Christians at Jerusalem were so poor at this time. Perhaps some blame for their poverty was related to the use of poor financial practices. The poverty may have been the result of a famine mentioned in Acts 11:28. It could be that those from foreign countries who had come to Jerusalem for Pentecost, had stayed on for a long time, and this was an added financial strain on the community.

At any rate, the need in Jerusalem was so great that Paul had exhorted the Christians in the churches of Galatia to also contribute financial aid.

(16:2) On the first day of the week let each one of you lay something aside, storing up as he may prosper, that there be no collections when I come.

The use of the phrase "on the first day of the week" suggests that Sunday had become the day when Christians were accustomed to meeting for worship (Acts 20:7). They were to set aside some money each week for the purpose of aiding those with special needs, so that when Paul arrived at Corinth it would not be necessary to lift offerings and appeal for funds.

The early church leaders were concerned that the people of God care for and support one another in time of need. They desired that the poor should be remembered (Galatians 2:10).

(16:3-4) And when I come, whomever you approve by your letters I will send to bear your gift to Jerusalem. But if it is fitting that I go also, they will go with me.

The Corinthian believers were to select worthy persons to carry the money-gift to the church at Jerusalem. They would carry letters indicating that they were approved by the local church for the task.[97]

Paul may accompany the envoys to Jerusalem if it seems fitting that he should go along. Christian leaders today must (like Paul) be especially careful about financial accountability, and not be haphazard in dealing with money matters.

It is instructive to note that Paul says nothing about a tithe. But he does make it clear that giving is to be proportionate to one's income. The Lord expects us to give

---

[97] Brethren writer, L. W. Teeter, says, "These letters were similar to the modern power of attorney, authorizing certain tried, safe, brethren to carry their bounty from the church at Corinth to the church at Jerusalem" (*New Testament Commentary*, page149).

generously (2 Corinthians 9:6-7), but we must determine the specific percentage. While believers in this age are not bound by the tithe, our giving under grace should not be less than the giving required under the law.

2. Prospective Journey Being Planned (16:5-9)

When we hope to visit friends, we sometimes write to them about our travel plans. That is what Paul did in this passage. He was writing from Ephesus, and was not yet certain about every detail of the journey. When he does arrive, he would stay with them perhaps during the winter.

(16:5-8) Now I will come to you when I pass through Macedonia (for I am passing through Macedonia). And it may be that I will remain, or even spend the winter with you, that you may send me on my journey, wherever I go. For I do not wish to see you now on the way; but I hope to stay a while with you, if the Lord permits. But I will tarry in Ephesus until Pentecost.

Travel in the 21st century is vastly different from the way it was in Paul's day. The speed has increased, and the time has decreased; the means of travel is altogether different—but the guiding principle which governed Paul's travel plans ("if the Lord permits") should remain the same for us (verse 7b).

Paul states in these verses that he had in mind going through Macedonia (northern Greece) and visiting the churches that had resulted from his second missionary journey—and then coming to Corinth (in southern Greece) for a longer visit with the church there.

Paul stated that his immediate task is at Ephesus, and he will not be finished with his responsibility there until Pentecost (verse 8). Paul's words "that you may send me on my journey" (verse 6b) implied that his hope was that the Corinthians would send him on his way with their good wishes and prayers.

(16:9) For a great and effective door has opened to me, and there are many adversaries.

Paul indicates that a significant door of opportunity had opened for him to labor at Ephesus, but there was also a frightening amount of opposition to his work. We can get some insight into the level of opposition which developed at Ephesus by reading the account describing the outbreak of rioting in Acts 19.

3. Exhortations for Christian Workers (16:10-18)

As Paul concludes the letter to the church at Corinth, he makes reference to Timothy and Apollos, both of whom have been mentioned earlier in the epistle.

(16:10-12) Now if Timothy comes, see that he may be with you without fear; for he does the work of the Lord, as I also do. Therefore let no one despise him. But send him on his journey in peace, that he may come to me; for I am waiting for him with the brethren. Now concerning our brother Apollos, I strongly urged him to come to you with the brethren, but he was quite unwilling to come at this time; however, he will come when he has a convenient time.

Paul voices personal concern for the Corinthians, and was hopeful that Timothy would come and minister to the church at Corinth. He would come before Paul's return to Corinth, and if he did come, they were to cooperate with him as he tries to correct some of the difficulties in the church. They were to treat him properly, and hopefully he could bring the good news that things were improving in the church at Corinth.

Paul speaks also of Apollos (verse 12). Paul had explained earlier (in 1 Corinthians 3:6-8) that he and Apollos were of one mind and one spirit in their work for the Lord. Now he had urged Apollos to visit Corinth again, but Apollos felt that it would not be wise to go there at this time. Paul graciously said that Apollos would visit them at a time convenient to him.

(16:13-14) Watch, stand fast in the faith, be brave, be strong. Let all that you do be done with love.

Before continuing with other personal references, Paul gives several exhortations for God's people.

We are to *"watch"*—that is, we are to be alert, constantly vigilant and awake! We are to watch lest Satan devour us (1 Peter 5:8). We are to watch lest we fall into temptation (Mark 14:38). We are to watch lest we fall for the heresies of false teachers (2 Peter 2:1). Most important of all, we are to be watching for the Lord's Return (Matthew 24:42).

We are to *"stand fast"*—that is, we must hold firmly to the faith once for all delivered to the saints (Jude 3). We are to have a settled faith in the evangelical teachings of the Bible—including the ordinances, the principles, and the restrictions of the gospel. We are not to follow "every wind of doctrine" that blows our way.

We are to *"be brave"*—that is, we are to act like men. The Greek word *andrizesthe* stresses masculinity. The NIV translates the word, "Be men of courage." The word carries with it the idea of having the strength of purpose which enables us to carry out the mandates of Scripture. Joshua (in his farewell address to Israel) admonished the people to "be very *courageous*...[and] to do all that is written in the book of the law of Moses" (Joshua 23:6).

We are to *"be strong"*—that is, we are to focus on developing a robust character, and to be clear in our convictions. Paul one time said, "For when I am weak, then I am strong" (2 Corinthians 12:10). We *need* strength—to *overthrow* false ideas and systems of thought (2 Corinthians 10:3-4); *to get along with* other Christians humbly and helpfully (Philippians 2:2-4; 2 Corinthians 1:4); *to recognize temptations* speedily and *resist* them firmly (1 Corinthians 10:13); and *to stand up for the truth* without compromise (Romans 1:14-16; 16:25-27).

We are to "let all that you do be done with love"—that is, to seek the best even for those who may seek the worst for us. We are told in 1 Peter 4:8 to "have fervent love for one another." *Fervent love* means that our love is to be sincere, strong, and lasting—not merely exhibiting a common respect for others. *Fervent love* means that we love the unlovely, that we love in spite of insult, and that we show love even when love is not returned.

The *Living Bible* paraphrase of verse 14 renders the text in a helpful way: "Keep your eyes open for spiritual danger; stand true to the Lord; act like men; be strong; and whatever you do, do it with kindness and love."

(16:15-18) I urge you, brethren—you know the household of Stephanas, that it is the firstfruits of Achaia, and that they have devoted themselves to the ministry of the saints—that you also submit to such, and to everyone who works and labors with us. I am glad about the coming of Stephanas, Fortunatus, and Achaicus, for what was lacking on your part they supplied. For they refreshed my spirit and yours. Therefore acknowledge such men"

We may remember that the household of Stephanas had the distinction of having been baptized by Paul himself (1 Corinthians 1:16). They had since that time established a record of faithful service in the church at Corinth (verse 15b), yet the people in the local congregation seem to have failed to give them appropriate appreciation. They were instructed to "submit" to those who work and labor for the welfare of the church.

Paul was very glad for the coming of Stephanus, Fortunatus, and Achaicus (verse 17). It must have been a joy to be in the presence of these brothers from Corinth. Their conversation "refreshed" Paul's spirit, and the report they took back to Corinth encouraged the Christians there.

The church at Corinth, in spite of its problems, was interested enough in spiritual things to seek out Paul's counsel. Of the three men mentioned, only Stephanus is named elsewhere in the Bible (1 Corinthians 1:16).

4. The Salutation and Closing Words (16:19-24)

In this section Paul comes to the concluding paragraphs of the letter. His final words include personal greetings and a benediction.

(16:19) The churches of Asia greet you. Aquila and Priscilla greet you heartily in the Lord, with the church that is in their house.

Paul sends greetings to the church at Corinth from the churches of Asia. Paul was writing from Ephesus, which was the principal city of the region. The "Asia" mentioned here was the *province* of Asia, a region on the west coast of the present-day country of Turkey. The churches greeted one another from distant places.

Aquila and Priscilla were well known to the people of Corinth, for this is the couple with whom Paul had lived and worked when he first came to Corinth (Acts 18:1-3). They traveled with him when he left Corinth and went to Ephesus. They were a hospitable and thoughtful couple who were Paul's "fellow workers in Christ Jesus" (Romans 16:3). One time they even "risked their own necks" to save Paul's life (Romans 16:4). They had in some way exposed their lives to danger for the purpose of protecting Paul. It was in their home where the church at Ephesus met.

(16:20) All the brethren greet you. Greet one another with a holy kiss.

The admonition to "greet one another with a holy kiss" is not taken seriously by most Christians in the West today, yet it is one of the most easy to follow commands in the Bible, and is not hard to understand.[98] The word "holy" guards the kiss against misconceptions that could be leveled against the practice.

Observing the command to use the kiss as a form of greeting was restored by the Anabaptists[99] and Pietists[100] because they set out to practice the New Testament "as it reads." They kept in mind of course the laws of proper Bible interpretation. The Anabaptists and Pietists honestly tried to take the Bible for what it says, and did not seek ways to detour around it or to re-interpret it. Brethren historian, Donald Durnbaugh, says, "The important thing was implicit obedience to all of Christ's commandments, even if they seemed insignificant" (*Brethren Beginnings:*

---

[98] Brethren writer, Peter Nead, wrote: "I will venture to say that we have not, in the Bible or Testament, a plainer command of anything, than that of the observance of the holy kiss" (*Primitive Christianity*, page 120).

[99] The Mennonite writer, J. C. Wenger, quotes from one of the early encyclopedias of theology (the *Catholic Encyclopedia*). It says, "From a very early date, the abuses to which this form of salutation might lead were very carefully guarded against. Both in the East and the West, women and men were separated in the assemblies of the faithful, and the kiss of peace was given only by women to women, and by men to men" (*Separated Unto God*, page 216).

[100] In the book, *The Old Brethren*, we read, "The kiss and the hand (called together the salutation) were used often...members greeted each other with it at meetings and elsewhere. At baptism, those on the shore greeted the new members thus as they came up from the water. It was used when a deacon was installed, when a minister was elected or ordained, and after the feet-washing. Its most profound use was before the bread and cup. On this occasion the Brethren recalled Christ's suffering and, not knowing when they might suffer likewise, they bound themselves together to be true to one another even in tribulation" (*The Old Brethren*, page 84).

The Origin of the Church of the Brethren in Eighteenth Century Europe, page 27).

(16:21-24) The salutation with my own hand—Paul's. If anyone does not love the Lord Jesus Christ, let him be accursed. O Lord, come! The grace of our Lord Jesus Christ be with you. My love be with you all in Christ Jesus. Amen.

It was the practice for Paul to dictate his letters, but now he takes the pen himself and writes a few closing lines in his own hand writing (verse 21). Paul concludes the letter with a note of spiritual hope and with expressions of esteem for the converts at Corinth.

The words "let him be accursed" (verse 22) are a strong warning about the consequence of failing to love the Lord Jesus Christ. The last word (a single word in the Greek) before the benediction is "O Lord, come!"[101] If there are other ways of salvation (beside faith in Jesus Christ), why should Paul say that if you don't love Jesus you shall be accursed?

Paul *began* the letter by wishing his readers the blessing of God's grace (1:3), and he *ends it* on the same note (16:23). These are not mere empty words. Paul knows that the church lives and labors and survives only by the sustaining grace of God.

Paul concludes the letter by assuring the believers at Corinth of his love. The epistle closes on a very tender note—"My love be with you all in Christ Jesus."

It is important to remember that when we believe in Christ Jesus, *we are not usually transformed instantly* into something totally different from what we had been before.

---

[101] The Greek words "Anathema" and "Maranatha" (left untranslated in the King James Version) mean "Let him be accursed at the coming of the Lord." The words "Our Lord comes" (Maranatha) were often used as a greeting among Christians in early centuries.

We are "a new creation" (2 Corinthians 5:17), but we need to "grow in the grace and knowledge of our Lord and Savior Jesus Christ" (2 Peter 3:18). The book of First Corinthians focuses on the sanctification of those who have believed in the Lord Jesus.

Paul's final words, "The grace of our Lord Jesus Christ be with you," are an expression of his prayer that God's undeserved kindness would be experienced in their lives day after day. The Corinthian letter must have been hard to write. It dealt with difficult issues and with sins that needed to be corrected, but Paul concludes with the words, "My love be with you all."

REVIEW QUESTIONS
Book of 1 Corinthians

1. The believers at Corinth were called "saints"—which means "holy" (1:2). As we read through the epistle, we sense that the people hardly fit the common definition of a saint. What are some of the characteristics of "saints"?

2. How can the church demonstrate the fact that the gospel message is for those whom our society thinks are important and prominent, as well as for those whom the world thinks are common and ordinary persons (1:26-28)?

3. Define (or give examples of) "the wisdom of God" and the "wisdom of this age" and contrast the two concepts (2:6-7).

4. The Christians at Corinth were causing divisions in the church by catering to and favoring certain leaders (3:4-8). How are divisions caused in our churches today?

5. Paul was very clear in stating that it is necessary to exercise church discipline (5:1-2, 13). Why are churches so hesitant to exercise church discipline in our day?

6. For what types of actions does your church impose discipline?

7. What are some of the approaches Christians might use to settle disputes between fellow-believers in our day (6:4-6)?

8. Read 6:1-8 and then consider what action you might take concerning a past due debt that is owed to you by a fellow Christian.

9. Are there some instances when Christians may need to have the law courts decide upon certain interpretations of the law? What might be some examples?

10. The Christian church pretty much stands alone in insisting on the permanence of marriage (7:10-11). What are some steps we can take to continue the emphasis on the permanence of marriage? List some of the attitudes and influences that are leading to the breakup of marriages.

11. Paul writes about "remaining in the same calling" we had occupied when we were called into the kingdom (7:20). What things change and what things remain the same when a person becomes a Christian? What occupations and/or professions are *unsuitable* for Christians?

12. Paul explains that if eating food that was once offered to idols caused a brother to stumble, he would refrain from eating it (8:13). Name some ethical decisions today which may cause a brother or sister to stumble.

13. Certain actions are considered "sin" by some people, while other believers consider the same actions to be acceptable behavior (10:23-24). How can two Christians who differ remain in the same congregation and continue to love each other?

14. How will you explain the critic who says that a head covering is unnecessary because *the hair* is the covering (11:15)? And what response should a sincere Christian give to those who say the head covering was merely a cultural practice (11:8-9)?

15. The communion service in the early church was observed in the context of a larger service known as the lovefeast (11:20-23). Write down your thoughts about some of the personal spiritual benefits of observing the lovefeast and communion services.

16. There are a number of kinds of spiritual gifts (12:4-11). How can we identify the spiritual gifts which we have? Where else in the New Testament can we find lists of spiritual gifts? What are some of the gifts not named in First Corinthians?

17. List some examples of times when the agape love of 1 Corinthians 13 ruled in your life.

18. Can you describe the difference between the gift of tongues and the gift of prophecy (14:2-3)? List some reasons why you believe that one or the other gift is the more important.

19. Browse through *the sermons* in the book of Acts and make note of all the references to the resurrection of Christ.

20. If you were to learn for sure that the resurrection of Christ was a hoax (15:13-19), how would that affect your personal life from day to day?

21. Read 16:10-24 and then describe steps that your church could take to encourage deeper bonds of friendship and compassion among Christians.

22. What are some of the primary lessons that you have learned from your study of the book of 1 Corinthians?

SELECTED BIBLIOGRAPHY
1 Corinthians

Anders, Max, ed. *Holman New Testament Commentary: I & II Corinthians*. Nashville: Broadman &Holman Publishers, 2000.

Barclay, William. *The Letters to the Corinthian: Daily Bible Study Series.* Philadelphia: Westminster Press, 1954.

Barclay, William. *Turning to God*. Philadelphia: Westminster Press, 1964.

Barnes, Albert. *Barnes' Notes on the New Testament: 1 Corinthians*. Grand Rapids: Baker Book House, 1962.

Bittinger, Emmert F. *Heritage and Promise:Perspectives on the Church of the Brethren.* Elgin, IL: Brethren Press, 1983.

Blair, J. Allen. *Living Wisely: A Devotional Study of the First Epistle to the Corinthians*. Neptune, NJ: Loizeaux Brothers, 1969.

Blomberg, Craig. *The NIV Application Commentary: 1 Corinthians*. Grand Rapids: Zondervan Publishing House, 1995.

Bowman, Carl F. *Brethren Society: The Cultural Transformation of a Peculiar People.* Baltimore:The Johns Hopkins University Press, 1995.

Bowman, Carl F. & Stephen L. Longenecker, eds. *Anabaptist Currents: History in Conversation with the Present*. Camden, Maine: Penobscot Press, 1995.

Brethren Life and Thought, Volume XIV, Number 2, Spring, 1969. Oak Brook, IL: Brethren Journal Association.

Cornes, Andrew. *Divorce & Remarriage: Biblical Disciplines and Pastoral Practice*. Grand Rapids: Eerdmans, 1984.

Durnbaugh, Donald F., ed. *The Brethren Encyclopedia (3 Volumes).* Elgin, IL: The Brethren Press, 1983.

Durnbaugh, Donald F. *The Brethren in Colonial America*. Elgin, IL: The Brethren Press, 1967.

Durnbaugh, Donald F. *Brethren Beginnings: The Origin of the Church of the Brethren in the Eighteenth Century.* Elgin, IL:The Brethren Press, 1958.

Dyck, Cornelius J. *Spiritual Life in Anabaptism*. Scottdale, PA: Herald Press, 1995.

Hershberger, Guy F., ed. *The Recovery of the Anabaptist Vision*. Scottdale, PA: Herald Press, 1957.

Kauffman, Daniel, Ed. *Doctrines of the Bible*. Scottdale, PA: Mennonite Publishing House, 1952.

Kurtz, D. W., Blough, S. S., Ellis, C. C. *Studies in Doctrine and Devotion*. Elgin, IL: Brethren Publishing House, 1919.

Lehman, James. *The Old Brethren. Elgin, IL: The Brethren Press, 1976.*

MacArthur, John, Jr. *The MacArthur New Testament Commentary: 1 Corinthians*. Chicago: Moody Press, 1984.

Mallott, Floyd E. *Studies in Brethren History*. Elgin, IL: Brethren Publishing House, 1954.

Mare, W. Harold. *The Expositor's Bible Commentary:1Corinthians (Volume 10)*. Frank E. Gaebelein, Editor. Grand Rapids: Zondervan, 1976.

"Men, Women, and Order in the Church," a sermon by John Calvin, translated by Seth Skolnitsky. Dallas, TX: Presbyterian Heritage Publications, 1992.

Minutes of the Annual Meetings of the Church of the Brethren: 1778-1909. General Mission Board. Elgin, IL: Brethren Publishing House, 1909.

Minutes of the Annual Conference of the Church of the Brethren: 1923-1944, compiled and edited by H. L. Hartsough, J. E. Miller, and Ora W. Garber. Elgin, IL: Brethren Publishing House, 1946.

Minutes of the Annual Conference of the Church of the Brethren: 1955-1964, compiled and edited by Ora W. Garber. Elgin, IL: Brethren Press, 1965.

Moore, J. H. *The New Testament Doctrines*. Elgin, IL: Brethren Publishing House, 1915.

Myer, James F. "The Plural Non-salaried Ministry" in *BRF Witness* Vol. 10, No. 2. Box 543, Ephrata, PA, 1975.

Nead, Peter. *Primitive Christianity*. Staunton, Virginia: Kenton Harper, 1834.

Packer, J. I. *Concise Theology*. Wheaton, IL: Tyndale House Publishers, 1993.

Sanseri, Gary. *Covered or Uncovered*. Milwaukee, OR: Back Home Industries, 1999.

Schaff, Philip. *History of the Christian Church* (8 volumes). New York, Scribners, 1910. (Reprint, 1960, Eerdmans).

Shaffer, Kenneth M. and Snyder, Graydon F. *Texts in Transit II.* Elgin, IL: Brethren Press, 1991.

Shank, Tom. *Let Her Be Veiled*, 2nd Edition. Eureka, MT: Torch Publications, 1991.

Shetler, Sanford G. & Shank, J. Ward. *Symbols of Divine Order in the Church*. Harrisonburg, VA: Sword & Trumpet, 1983.

Shetler, Sanford G. *Paul's Letter to the Corinthians*. Harrisonburg, VA: Christian Light Publications, 1971.

Stoffer, Dale R. *Background and Development of Brethren Doctrines 1650-1987*. Philadelphia: Brethren Encyclopedia, Inc., 1989.

Stover, Wilbur. A tract "Why I Love My Church" in *Brethren Tracts and Pamphlets*. Elgin, IL: Brethren Publishing House, 1900.

Teeter, L. W. *New Testament Commentary in Two Volumes*. Mount Morris, IL: The Brethren's Publishing Co., 1894.

Thayer, J. H. *Greek-English Lexicon of the New Testament*. Edinburgh, Scotland, T. & T. Clark, Fourth Ed. 1901.

The Analytical Greek Lexicon. (no author and no date given). New York: Harper & Brothers.

Wenger, J. C. *God's Word Written: Essays on the Nature of Biblical Revelation, Inspiration, and Authority*. Scottdale, PA: Herald Press, 1966.

Wenger, J. C. *Separated Unto God: A Plea for Christian Simplicity in Life and for a Scriptural Nonconformity to the World.* Scottdale, PA: Herald Press, 1955.

Winger, Otho. *History and Doctrines of the Church of the Brethren*. Elgin, IL: Brethren Publishing House, 1920.

MANCHESTER COLLEGE LIBRARY

3 9315 01048838 2

227.2 M364f
Martin, Harold S., 1930-
1 Corinthians

DATE DUE

WITHDRAWN
from
Funderburg Library